Mushrooms on the Menu

MUSHROOMS ON THE MENU

JOHN MIDGLEY

AURUM PRESS

PUBLISHER'S NOTE

This book is not intended for identification purposes and neither the Author nor the Publishers accept any liability for any cases of poisoning caused by eating wild mushrooms. Never eat any that have not been positively identified as safe by an expert and always use a reliable field guide. If ever in any doubt whatsoever about a mushroom's identity, leave it alone.

First published 1993 by Aurum Press Limited, 25 Bedford Avenue, London WC1B 3AT

A catalogue record for this book is available from the British Library.

ISBN 1 85410 255 9

10 9 8 7 6 5 4 3 2 1
1997 1996 1995 1994 1993

Illustrations and design by Don Macpherson
Cover photograph by Matthew Ward
Typeset by York House Typographic Ltd
Printed in Great Britain by Hartnolls Ltd, Bodmin

For my family, especially Sue

CONTENTS

INTRODUCTION

I could have written this book twice over, with recipes to spare – that's how delicious mushrooms are!

As it is, I am content to share the following recipes – 120 or so in all. Reflecting my own preferences and tastes (and those of my family) they represent several different culinary traditions – Asian, Mediterranean and central European. At home we are as likely to cook with oriental equipment, ingredients and techniques as we are with more familiar ones. Our catholic tastes have evolved from years of experimentation with recipes and from a desire to recreate at home some of the delicious things we have enjoyed in more exotic surroundings. As a keen bibliophile with a passion for cookery books, as an obsessive, self-taught cook, and as the son of well-travelled parents who appreciated good food, I can truthfully claim never to have suffered from a jaded palate.

Although there are some quite substantial dishes of meat and game, for the most part the recipes are reasonably light. A large section is dedicated to pasta, which combines equally well with wild and cultivated mushrooms. The bulk of the book is devoted to little dishes; first courses and light meals; pasta; soups; salads; vegetable accompaniments; and preserves. Many of the first courses are also suitable as complete light meals, and most of the antipasti, canapés, hors d'œuvres and tapas can be served in first courses when entertaining. I have also included some of the classic one-pot or all-in-one dishes of the mushroom repertoire which invariably are very good cooked at home but sometimes suffer in restaurant kitchens.

Although cheaper cuts of meat are specified when appropriate (in stews, for example), luxury cuts of loin and fillet are required in a few recipes. This is because we eat meat relatively infrequently and like to treat ourselves when we do. Nor do I eschew currently unfashionable ingredients such as butter, wine and cream. They are important in

French mushroom cookery, in particular, and do no harm if they are indulged in occasionally within a varied and interesting diet. There are many more recipes in this book that are prepared with healthy olive oil, garlic and the complex carbohydrates in bread, pasta and rice.

Nobody who has eaten ceps and morels is likely to forget the experience, and I have included several recipes for those wild delicacies. However, I have not focussed exclusively on wild mushrooms. For those who have caught the bug, there are recipes within these covers that show you how to deal with your wild mushrooms. Recently, I have encountered many more intrepid Britons out and about in search of edible fungi than I would have believed likely two or three years ago. (Continental Europeans resident in this country jealously keep their hunting grounds a closely guarded secret.)

Although we are waking up to the joy of ceps and other edible fungi, most people remain deeply suspicious of the funny-looking 'toadstools' that they encounter on walks. For that reason, and in recognition of the availability of oyster and shiitake mushrooms in the supermarkets – not to mention white and chestnut-coloured mushrooms in their closed-, open- and flat-capped stages of maturity – virtually every recipe in this book can be prepared with cultivated mushrooms. You will find, however, that a regular store of dried ceps and morels will allow you to improve the flavour of the cultivated varieties; although the commercial ones are expensive, they stretch a long way and their dark, concentrated soaking liquid is also used.

Finally, I have only included one truffle recipe – for the more affordable English summer truffle, at that. Périgord and Alba truffles are quite beyond most people's pockets and perhaps are best enjoyed in restaurants that specialize in northern Italian dishes or the cuisine of Périgord and Provence. However, Italian white truffle oil, though expensive, lasts a long time and manages to capture the bewitching aroma of the fungus; only a few drops will transform a dish totally.

Serving suggestions and quantities accompany each recipe.

Good hunting and bon appetit!

A BRIEF CULINARY HISTORY OF MUSHROOMS

Mushrooms and truffles are extremely ancient foods. Evidence exists that truffles were eaten in large quantities by the Babylonians, but edible fungi were almost certainly gathered many thousands of years earlier by our distant ancestors.

The ancient Greeks and Romans knew several edible fungi and may even have managed to cultivate some species. Our word mycology derives from the Greek μυκης (a blob of mucus, from which mushrooms were believed to be formed). The Romans classified mushrooms according to their physical resemblance to other things: the fat-stemmed, fleshy boleti were *suilli* ('swine-like'), whereas the gilled agarics and amanitas were *boleti*, or 'little lumps'. Modern Italians retain the swine analogy, calling the excellent *Boletus edulis* species and its close relatives, *Boletus aereus*, *Boletus aestivalis* and *Boletus pinicola*, porcini ('little pigs'). *Amanita caesarea* was favoured by Roman Emperors, and wicked Agrippina murdered the Emperor Claudius by lacing his favourite dish of Caesar's mushrooms with morsels of the deadly *Amanita phalloides* (death cap). Among Pompeii's beautiful frescoes is a lovingly rendered edible mushroom that is identifiable as *Lactarius deliciosus*. Apicius's cookery book includes a recipe for truffles stewed in olive oil, fermented fish sauce, black pepper, wine and honey. Our word mushroom almost certainly derives from the late Latin *moussiriones*, via French *mousserons*, with a distant root in Greek μυκης. *Mousseron* survives as the French name for St George's and fairy ring mushrooms.

Emperors and peasants alike have eaten wild mushrooms for centuries, the former through choice, the latter out of necessity. Japanese and Chinese cooks have long valued many kinds of mushrooms, such as *Lentinus edodes* (shiitake, which means 'forest mushroom' in Japanese, also known as Chinese black fungus); *Volvariella esculenta* (paddy-straw mushroom); *Flammulina velutipes* (enokitake, or velvet shank);

Dictyophora indusiata (bamboo fungus); several kinds of *Pleurotus* (oyster mushroom); *Tricholoma matsutake* (matsutake, or pine mushroom); and various jelly fungi, including *Auricularia auricula-judae* (cloud ear, Jew's ear fungus).

Russians, Poles and Scandinavians, in particular, have always relied upon wild mushrooms which while in season are eaten fresh, then preserved by drying, salting and pickling. In fact, throughout Europe peasants depended on wild foods to supplement their dreary diet. Ironically, such ingredients have become highly coveted luxury foods. Truffles were largely ignored in France until they acquired a reputation as an aphrodisiac in the fourteenth century. Many explanations for their alleged aphrodisiac qualities have been offered; the most convincing is their frankly rude smell, which attracts sows and bitches. Since Roman times, these animals have been used to sniff them out. Truffles' aroma is very similar to the scent secreted by wild boars. It is said that human virgins were once employed to locate truffles by smell, a practice outlawed by the Church. The popularity and price of truffles really took off in the nineteenth century and have continued to soar ever since. A similar fate has befallen the best species of edible wild mushrooms such as ceps, morels and chanterelles.

Fungi have also played a more sinister role in human nutrition, causing massive outbreaks of poisoning and famine by infecting cereal crops. Ergotism first afflicted Germany in 857, with disastrous consequences. All cereals are susceptible to smuts and rusts and *Claviceps purpurea* (rye ergot) can contaminate grains so severely that even the intense heat of the bread oven fails to destroy its cocktail of toxins, inducing in its victims a host of terrible symptoms, including dementia, acute skin inflammation leading to gangrene, and death. (One such toxin is lysergic acid diethylamide – LSD; others cause severe abdominal pain.) The condition's vernacular names of 'holy fire' and 'St Anthony's fire' refer to the victims' hot, inflamed skin, to the acceptance of the affliction as divine punishment and to the belief that St Anthony could intercede on behalf of supplicants.

Mushroom cultivation ensured a consistent supply which in turn boosted demand. Shiitake were first cultivated over a thousand years ago in southern China but the most significant development was the taming of an agaric that still accounts for nearly all of the world's output.

In 1678, a French botanist by the name of Marchant discovered that the mycelial strands of wild *Agaricus bisporus* would continue to produce mushrooms when transferred to a suitable growing medium. Manure-enriched compost, used by market gardeners in disused quarries near Paris to grow Mediterranean fruits and vegetables, was the perfect growing medium. The hot beds already produced naturally occurring crops of mushrooms, but following Marchant's discovery the growers realized that a year-round crop of hitherto seasonal wild mushrooms could be maintained. To this day, *Agaricus bisporus* is also known as the *champignon de Paris*.

The annual global production of cultivated mushrooms is nearly 2 million tonnes, the vast majority (99.5 per cent in Britain in 1992) *Agaricus bisporus*. Others include *Lentinus edodes* (shiitake), *Volvariella esculenta* (paddy-straw mushroom), *Pleurotus ostreatus* (oyster mushroom) and other 'exotics', as they are termed in the trade. The leading producing nation is the USA, although EC countries, especially France, Britain and Holland, and oriental producers such as China and South Korea are also important growers.

Advances in cultivation

Great progress has been made during the last six years or so in the wider cultivation of edible wild species. Growers in many different countries cultivate a tastier, brown-capped strain of *Agaricus bisporus* called the chestnut mushroom, as well as *Lentinus edodes* and *Pleurotus ostreatus*. Given the right temperature, light and humidity, pretty yellow *Pleurotus cornucopiae*, pink *pleurotus salmoneos-tramineus*, and brown *pleurotus cajor-aju* (all related to oyster mushrooms) can be grown at home in bags that can be acquired by mail order from enterprising growers (see Useful Addresses). These mushrooms can also be found on the vegetable shelves in large supermarket chains.

A stunning exhibition of oyster, shiitake and other mushrooms staged by Wentworth Exotic Mushrooms at the 1992 Chelsea Flower Show attracted unprecedented public interest, chiefly, one suspects, of the morbid kind. Seen through the eyes of fuchsia fanciers and laburnum lovers, fungi are objects of fear and loathing. ('Ugh – are those *mushrooms*?' I overheard an elderly lady question her gentleman companion with eloquent distaste.) Gardeners with mycological leanings may like to visit a new, experimental 'Fungus Garden' recently created by Dr Roy Watling in Edinburgh's Royal Botanic Garden.

Lepista nuda (wood blewit), *Armillaria mellea* (honey fungus), *Lepiota procera* (parasol mushroom), *Flammulina velutipes* (velvet shank), *Sparassis crispa* (cauliflower fungus) and *Grifola frondosa* (hen of the woods) can now be cultivated successfully; perhaps, eventually, such highly prized fungi as ceps, chanterelles, morels and truffles will be tamed by the mushroom growers who anticipate a potentially lucrative market.

How mushrooms grow

Fungi are among the most primitive, diverse and successful of life forms. Fossilized fungi over one thousand million years old have been found in Precambrian rocks. Lacking chlorophyll, they do not qualify strictly as plants, and rely upon other materials in order to feed and grow. Their range is huge, with approximately 1.6 million species (more than the plant and animal kingdoms). These include the beneficial yeasts needed for brewing and bread-making; life-saving penicillin and other antibiotics; less appetizing micro-organisms that are responsible for dry rot, athlete's foot, thrush and ringworm; insect- or air-born moulds, rusts and mildews afflicting crops and trees; lichens (fungi co- existing symbiotically with algae); and the many thousands of 'higher' mushrooms and so-called 'toadstools'. All fungi obtain their nutrients in symbiotic relationships with other organisms, be they living or dead wood, leaf litter, animal excrement, or dead or living animal tissue.

However, not all fungi are merely parasitic, since some and their hosts are inter-dependent. This is particularly true of fungi that grow in mycorrhizal relationships with the roots of trees and plants. This relationship is defined by mycologists as 'a mutualistic symbiosis between certain soil fungi and plant roots'. *Leccinum versipelle, Leccinum quercinum* and *Leccinum aurantiacum*, for example, will only be found close to birch, oak and aspen, respectively, and actually prevent dangerous fungi from attacking their hosts by forming an impenetrable shield around their roots, while helping them to absorb nutrients from the soil. In general, however, the invaluable role that fungi share with bacteria is to promote decay and to dispose of organic materials, acting as nature's recyclers by reclaiming their nutrients for the soil.

Despite the absence of chlorophyll, mushrooms may be likened in most other regards to plants. What we see are merely the temporary fruiting bodies of an invisible or partly obscured plant lurking beneath the surface of wood, leaf litter or soil, or entwined with the root systems of trees and shrubs. The permanent part of the plant is the *mycelium*, a network of tiny threads from which the mushrooms or toadstools emerge when prompted by the right combination of stimuli. The sole, urgent purpose of these fruiting bodies is to produce and disperse spores for reproduction. Seen thus, the mushrooms that we gather and eat are like berries and other fruits; provided that we pick them carefully, without disturbing the mycelium or damaging it by over-collection, we do not endanger the living organism.

When the right conditions of humidity, warmth (or a sudden drop in temperature), light and nutrition coincide, the mycelium sprouts bud-like growths which in some cases are capable of very rapid growth, progressing from pin-heads to mature, then convex and finally flat or concave caps supported by vertical stems. The characteristic mushroom shape is designed to protect the spores harboured in the gills or pores from rain, performing exactly the same function as an umbrella.

The spores are released in different ways. Puffballs and earthballs expel their spores by bursting open when ruptured by the impact of rain drops; others are carried and dispersed by the insects and small mammals that nibble on or walk over them; others still are carried away on the breeze. Whatever the means of dispersal, some will find the right conditions to germinate in a new place and will begin to form a new mycelium from microscopic filaments known as *hyphae*. When a new mycelium meets and entwines with another of the same species, new fruiting bodies will emerge when the right external stimuli are recreated.

The higher fungi belong to either of two groups that are characterized by their spore-producing mechanisms. The *Ascomycetes* are the larger and more primitive of the two, producing shooting spores in tiny flask-like containers known as *asci*. Morels and truffles are the most illustrious Ascomycetes but most of the thirty thousand member species are very small organisms such as yeasts. *Basidiomycetes* are a much more familiar group with some thirteen thousand species carrying their spores at the end of thousands of little protuberances called *basidia*. Agarics (gilled fungi), boleti (pored fungi), bracket fungi, jelly fungi, puffballs, chanterelles, cauliflower fungus and hedgehog fungus, among others, belong to this group.

Mushrooms in the environment

Whether they protect or damage their hosts, fungi are essential components of a balanced environment. Honey fungus, though a feared foe of foresters and gardeners because it spreads virulently through connective black filaments called *rhizomorphs* from infected material to healthy trees and shrubs, is a natural inhibitor. *Armillaria* have evolved over millions of years and in the course of evolution have controlled forests. A single *Armillaria bulbosa* network which may be the world's largest and oldest living organism was recently discovered growing in a forest in Michigan, spread out over an area of at least 15 hectares, weighing some 100 tonnes (as much as a blue whale) and reckoned to have been alive for 1500 years!

Many other fungi form *mycorrhizal* associations with the root systems of trees and plants and help them to absorb moisture and nutrients, especially where the soil is poor or very acid. Approximately 90 per cent of flowering plants, including grasses, crops and fruit trees, all forest trees in the northern hemisphere and many tropical trees, form *mycorrhizae*. Perversely, modern crop-spraying destroys the beneficial fungi that promote growth and provide root protection *as well as* harmful rusts and smuts.

Most mushrooms and toadstools only thrive in clean, unpolluted environments, so their very presence is reassuring. Unfortunately, however, they readily absorb radioactive materials from the soil and, once contaminated by radioactive leakage or fall-out, will pass these on to humans who eat them. The Chernobyl accident badly contaminated many wooded areas. Some governments, including Italy, have banned dried wild mushrooms from affected areas.

Since the distribution of fungi is partly determined by climate, global warming may affect populations. Morels and summer truffles, for example, are decidedly rare in Britain, favouring the warmer southern counties, while delicious *Tuber magnatum* (Alba truffle), *Tuber melanosporum* (Périgord truffle), *Amanita caesarea* (Caesar's mushroom) and others have not yet crossed the Channel. Since there is some evidence that global warming has already started however, even these fungi may yet reach Britain.

Mushroom hunting

Hunting for edible fungi is traditional in many European countries. Whole families join in the fun, armed with stout sticks, wicker baskets and sharp knives to sever the fungi from wood or soil. Such is the enthusiasm for mushroom hunting in Russia, for example, that the start of the season in mid-July is called *hodit' po griby* ('finding the mushroom'). All Moscow sets off to find mushrooms in the forests of pine, birch and aspen, a beloved activity that is vividly and frequently recorded in Russian literature. Scandinavians, Poles, Hungarians, Germans, Swiss, Italians, French and Catalans, to name but a few, are equally fanatical hunters.

By contrast, the British have lost touch with a food-foraging tradition that survives only in berry-picking. Although until the nineteenth century some wild species such as blewits and field mushrooms were available in country markets, this suspicious attitude is deep-seated. Fear of poisoning alone fails to explain it. Many people call all but a couple of species of higher fungi 'toadstools', reserving the term 'mushroom' for field mushrooms and the familiar ones available in shops and supermarkets. The dictionary definition of toadstool is a poisonous or inedible mushroom-shaped fungus. Yet of the thousand or so species found in Britain, only about fifty are poisonous, of which the really dangerous fungi can be counted on two hands; only eight or nine common ones are considered deadly.

Television coverage and the regular appearances on cookery programmes by mushroom gourmets such as the avuncular Antonio Carluccio, and the reams of space that have been devoted to wild mushrooms recently in glossy magazines and the food pages of national newspapers have prompted many more people to head for the woods and fields in search of fungi for the pot.

My advice to anyone contemplating a mushroom hunt would be first to join a foray led by an expert, not only to avoid potentially lethal – though unlikely – errors but also to learn the basic techniques of identification and subsequently to apply them with confidence. Since the key aspects by which species are identified vary considerably according to age, humidity and recent rainfall, novices are unlikely to do very well without some expert guidance. Once safely encountered, species will be recognized again far more readily than if the only available references have been the pages of a book. Several organizations (see Useful Addresses) conduct forays, including local natural history societies, the Wildlife Partnership Trust and the British Mycological Society, an academic body that welcomes associate members from outside the groves of academe. BMS's monthly magazine, *The Mycologist*, publishes advance details of forays held all over the country. The Field Studies Council runs residential fungi identification courses at several of its centres.

The essential equipment for a foray are a sharp knife, a wicker basket and warm, weather-proof clothing and footwear. Although many habitats harbour edible fungi, the most likely are ancient woodland (broad-leaved, mixed and pine woods all provide a home to a wide variety of species), old pastures (especially if well-manured by horses, cows and sheep), downs, heaths, and even urban parks and gardens. Indeed, any habitat that is not swampy or where the ground vegetation has not taken a stranglehold should, in the right conditions and season, yield edible mushrooms. Mushrooms appear more readily soon after rain or during spells of high humidity, so dry summers and autumns are less productive than wet ones.

It is also well worth getting to know your trees since mushrooms grow on or near to different species. Some, such as cauliflower fungus, grow exclusively from the submerged roots or stumps of conifers, especially Scots pine, while others, including ceps and the more common bay boletus, are less fussy and appear near several different tree species, especially birch, pine, oak, beech and sweet chestnut. You are much more likely to find wild oyster mushrooms on dead or dying beech and elm than on other timbers.

Although mushrooms are more abundant in the autumn, some make an earlier appearance, especially in warm, humid conditions following a good soaking, while others are only found in the spring.

Traditionally, mushroom pickers get up early to be first on the scene, and many mushrooms are freshest then. Avoid collecting soon after rain as the mushrooms will be waterlogged. Collect only moderate quantities to protect the mycelium and the specimens at the bottom of your basket! When picking, pull the whole fruiting body up first as the base is sometimes a vital clue to identification. Once you have identified the mushroom, slice off the stem base. Severing the mushroom from the ground at the base does not protect the mycelium; on the contrary, the stump may rot and infect the mycelium.

Pick only perfect specimens, avoiding any that seem limp, maggoty, unnaturally soft or old. If the cut stem is riddled with little holes, or if holes are visible on the gills or caps, as is all too frequently the case with oyster mushrooms, for example, maggots have moved in. (I make an exception for ceps, however, keeping maggoty specimens in a separate basket to prevent migration to my virgin mushrooms. I slice the infected ceps thinly for drying, and the maggots quickly evacuate their home as soon as the mushrooms begin to dehydrate.)

Catering for – and profiting hugely from – the growing international demand for wild mushrooms are the networks of professional mushroom pickers. Active in many different parts of the world, from the USA, France and Italy to tropical countries such as Zambia and Zimbabwe where chanterelles and other species abound, they are controlled and coordinated by central agents, most based in southern France, although one multi-million pound business is based in Scotland. They are dedicated to bringing wild mushrooms to market at all times of the year. Consequently, the determined gourmet may find ceps in prestige outlets well into the winter, and the brief availability of fresh morels has been bolstered by imported specimens picked in the pristine pastures of the Himalayas.

Common edible varieties

Some experts list nearly one hundred edible wild species, while other authorities are more selective, recommending between twenty and fifty that are good to eat. Good field guides give vital information on edibility and classify fungi as 'deadly', 'poisonous', 'edibility unknown', or 'edible'. Some books, especially those published in continental Europe, elaborate further, giving edible species star-ratings. The following listing of the top thirty or so native and reasonably common edible wild species is cautious, since I have excluded all the *Amanitas*, of which the few edible ones may easily be confused by the novice with their dangerous cousins. I have also excluded the *Russulas*, which the novice will struggle to differentiate (some are good to eat, others are inedible or emetic); the *Suillus* group of mushrooms and *Flammulina velutipes* which, though pleasantly flavoured, are unpalatably slimy; and very rare or alien species.

Botanical name	Common name
Agaricus arvensis	horse mushroom
Agaricus campestris	field mushroom
Armillaria mellea	honey fungus
Auricularia auricula-judae	Jew's ear fungus
Boletus badius	bay boletus
Boletus edulis	cep, penny bun
Cantharellus cibarius	chanterelle
Cantharellus infundibuliformis	winter chanterelle, yellow leg
Coprinus comatus	shaggy ink cap, lawyer's wig
Craterellus cornocopioides	horn of plenty, black trumpet
Fistulina hepatica	beefsteak fungus
Grifola frondosa	hen of the woods
Hydnum repandum	hedgehog fungus
Laccaria amethystea	amethyst deceiver
Laccaria laccata	deceiver
Lactarius deliciosus	saffron milk cap
Laetiporus sulphureus	chicken of the woods
Langermannia gigantea	giant puff ball
Leccinum scabrum	brown birch boletus
Leccinum versipelle	orange birch boletus
Lepiota procera	parasol mushroom
Lepiota rhacodes	shaggy parasol
Lepista nuda	wood blewit
Lepista saeva	field blewit, blue leg
Lycoperdon pratense, perlatum	puffballs
Marasmius oreades	fairy ring mushroom
Morchella (vulgaris, esculenta, elata, conica)	morels
Pleurotus cornucopiae	cornucopia mushroom
Pleurotus ostreatus	oyster mushroom

Polyporus squamosus	dryad's saddle
Sparassis crispa	cauliflower fungus
Tricholoma gambosum	St George's mushroom
Tuber aestivum	summer truffle
Volvariella bombycina	—

Mushrooms and nutrition

The common cultivated champignon is 91.5 per cent water. Nutrition-ally, mushrooms are of modest value although they are a good source of potassium, phosphorus, iron and copper; vitamins B_1, B_2, B_{12}, C, pantothenic acid and niacin; vegetable protein; and essential amino acids. They are low in salt, calories, carbohydrate and fat, and contain no cholesterol. Experimental studies have linked shiitake mushrooms, in particular, with the therapeutic effect of lowering blood cholesterol levels and reducing high blood pressure. For centuries, traditional eastern medicine has valued shiitake as 'the elixir of life'.

Cooking with mushrooms

Cultivated *Agaricus bisporus* buttons, small, tender *Pleurotus ostreatus*, *Pleurotus salmoneos-tramineus*, *Pleurotus cornucopiae* and a few wild species such as ceps and bay boleti in their firm, youthful state are delicious thinly sliced, dressed with lemon juice, finely chopped garlic and olive oil, and eaten raw. However, most species should be cooked; indeed, in some species such as *Armillaria mellea*, *Morchella vulgaris* and *Morchella esculenta*, cooking destroys mild toxins that are present in the raw fungus. The following golden rules will ensure that you get the best out of your mushrooms:

1. Never keep mushrooms longer than two or three days, even when refrigerated (store them in a paper bag in the vegetable drawer). Mushrooms spoil quickly and stale ones will be soft and unpleasant to smell and taste. Many wild mushrooms should be consumed within 24 hours, or preserved by drying, pickling or, in some cases, freezing.

2. Never cook with waterlogged mushrooms, so avoid collecting them after rain. Wild mushrooms tend to have a higher moisture content than cultivated ones and in all cases, the older the mushroom, the mushier it will be.

3. Virtually all varieties are very good sautéed in butter or olive oil with onions, shallots or garlic and fresh herbs (especially parsley and

thyme). I like to cook them over a fierce heat initially, to gild them, then more gently until they have shed their moisture and have reduced in bulk by up to forty per cent. To avoid burning the butter, I usually add some olive oil to the pan. This technique concentrates the natural mushroom flavour.

4. Mushrooms seem to have an affinity with the following ingredients: butter; garlic, shallots and onions; olive oil; parsley and thyme; potatoes; cream and soured cream; paprika; chilli; sweet peppers; eggs; pasta; rice; beans and pulses; bread and pastry; sherry and Madeira; acidic ingredients such as white wine, lemon juice and tomatoes. They are excellent with beef, poultry and all kinds of game.

5. Use good quality stock, especially in soups. Home-made stock is best (see recipe on p. 114).

6. The flavour of cultivated mushrooms is vastly enhanced by the addition of dried and reconstituted ceps or morels. The best ones come from Italy and France. Some delicatessens sell them loose, by weight, but they are more commonly available in little packets. Although these are very expensive, only small quantities are required – 12 g (½ oz) for recipes to serve four people; soak in a cup of hot water, allowing 20 minutes for ceps, 30 minutes for morels. Remove the mushrooms and strain the soaking liquid, which will have a deposit of sand and grit. Add the soaking liquid at the appropriate time and allow it to evaporate, though not, of course, in soups; this concentrates the flavour.

7. Cultivated mushrooms need little cleaning; any specks of growing compost may be wiped away with a cloth or with kitchen paper. Washing or rinsing will impair the flavour and turn them mushy. Most wild mushrooms should be wiped clean. The whole mushroom should be picked as the stem base is a vital clue to identification. Once the species is verified, sever the base while holding the mushroom with the cap facing up, otherwise the dirt particles will lodge in the gills or pores. The caps can be cleaned with a brush or cloth (specialist mushroom knives incorporate a brush). However, intricately lobed fungi such as morels and cauliflower fungus must be washed very thoroughly to remove grass, leaves, grit and pine needles.

8. Avoid bruising mushrooms and always store them above heavier foods in the shopping or collecting basket and in the refrigerator.

9. Cultivated *Agaricus bisporus* mushrooms are marketed in four stages of development: buttons; closed cap; open cap; and large, flat cap. The

first two are firm, suitable for marinating, and may be sliced, minced or cooked whole in sauces. Open cap mushrooms may be chopped or sliced and cooked in sauces and soups, or stuffed and grilled, or baked. Flat-cap mushrooms have the strongest flavour and are best grilled, baked or cooked in soups and sauces.

10. Others, such as shiitake and oyster mushrooms, can be sliced and cooked like any other mushrooms, and the former are distinctively flavoured. Dried oriental shiitake are rich and savoury, and the Japanese ones are usually considered superior to Chinese. The tough stalks should be removed after reconstitution in hot water and the caps very finely sliced; they are an essential ingredient in many oriental dishes.

Note on other ingredients

Most, if not all, of the ingredients are readily obtainable, either in larger branches of leading supermarkets or in delicatessens and ethnic food shops.

Tomato *passata*, for example, is merely sieved, bottled plum tomatoes; tinned plum tomatoes, briefly liquidized in a food processor, can be substituted. Extra virgin olive oil is often called for, especially to flavour dishes, whereas refined ('pure') olive oil is more suitable when the rather assertive flavour of the unrefined first pressing of olives is not desired (when frying, for example). Oriental ingredients such as fish sauce (also called *nam pla* if imported from Thailand) can be bought in Chinese and Asian supermarkets, although light soy sauce is an acceptable substitute.

A large section is devoted to pasta. There are three kinds. Good quality, fresh egg pasta can be made at home or bought from reputable Italian delicatessens that make a fresh supply daily. Other kinds of so-called 'fresh' pasta should be avoided as they are usually of poor quality. Egg pasta is also allowed to dry out, for indefinite storage. This kind can be bought in packets. Requiring a longer cooking time than fresh egg pasta, it tends to swell in the process so less is required. The third and most familiar pasta is *pasta di semola di grano duro* (factory-made durum wheat pasta). Whereas in the northern half of Italy egg pasta is preferred, the southern regions favour this kind. Very good brands include Agnesi, de Cecco, and Gerardo di Nola; I love their gaudy packaging. Durum wheat pasta is generally preferable to all but the best quality egg pasta, and goes very well with robust sauces and fungi. I suggest alternative pasta shapes in each recipe.

ANTIPASTI, CANAPÉS, HORS D'ŒUVRES, SNACKS AND TAPAS

Champiñones al ajillo

A popular tapa that is served in bars all over Spain. The mushrooms are cooked quickly to retain their juiciness. If you have a heat diffuser, you can cook this on top of the stove in a traditional Spanish clay *cazuela* (or in any earthenware pot); otherwise, use a well seasoned or non-stick frying pan with steep sides, and pour the cooked contents into preheated oven-proof serving dishes, to ensure that the mushrooms stay very hot. This serves four with a small selection of tapas and plenty of crusty bread to mop up the flavoured juices, or two as an appetizer.

350 g (12 oz) button mushrooms
110 ml (4 fl oz) olive oil
4 cloves of garlic, peeled and chopped (not too finely)
1 small dried red chilli
salt
generous handful of fresh parsley, washed and finely chopped

Trim the bottoms of the mushrooms' stems and wipe the caps clean. Slice them in half.

Heat the olive oil to smoking point. Throw in the mushrooms and toss them in the hot oil until they are lightly browned (about 3 minutes). Add the garlic and chilli and toss around for 30 seconds longer. Season, add the parsley, mix and serve immediately.

Setas a la plancha

I have tried to recreate some wonderful wild oyster mushrooms I once enjoyed as a tapa in Bar La Trucha, Madrid. Cultivated oyster mushrooms can be substituted, although they will taste blander. Serves four as an appetizer.

*450 g (1 lb) oyster
  mushrooms, left whole
110 g (4 oz) plain flour, for
  dusting
1 tsp salt*

*freshly milled black pepper
a pinch of cayenne pepper
110 ml (4 fl oz) olive oil
handful of fresh parsley,
  washed and chopped*

Clean the mushrooms by wiping or brushing away any dirt. Trim off all but the very top of the stems and, if using wild specimens, discard any with little maggot holes: the cut stems must be unperforated and white, not yellowing.

Heat a cast-iron pan or griddle. Meanwhile, mix the flour with the salt, plenty of black pepper and the cayenne and roll the mushrooms in the seasoned flour. Quickly dip them in the olive oil in batches and lay them on the hot surface. Turn them after a minute and sear again on the other side, taking care not to burn them. Sprinkle with parsley and serve hot.

Mushroom, bacon and mozzarella canapés

Mushrooms wrapped in bacon stay juicy. They can be served as fairly substantial canapés, or as a starter for four.

12 medium-sized button mushrooms	60 g (3 oz) mozzarella, finely diced
salt	12 bacon rashers
freshly milled black pepper	olive oil

Preheat the grill. Season each mushroom. Sprinkle the mozzarella over the bacon rashers. Place a seasoned mushroom at one end of each rasher of bacon. Wrap the mushrooms up in the bacon rashers, folding the ends over them. Drizzle a little olive oil over each and grill the canapés, turning once, until the bacon is almost crisp and the mozzarella has begun to ooze out of the sides. Serve hot.

Sautéed baby boleti

Ideally, use baby ceps, birch boleti, bay boleti or a combination. Alternatively, small, firm chestnut buttons can be substituted, although there will be some loss of flavour. Serving two, these mushrooms are also a good vegetable accompaniment to meat, poultry or game.

6 tbs olive oil	salt
350 g (12 oz) small, very firm boleti	freshly milled black pepper
3 cloves of garlic, peeled and finely chopped	handful of fresh parsley, washed and chopped
140 ml (5 fl oz) home-made chicken or vegetable stock (see recipe on p. 114)	

Heat the olive oil. Sear the boleti over a high heat for a minute. Reduce the heat, add the garlic and gently fry for 3–4 minutes longer. Add the stock, season and allow the liquid almost to evaporate. Sprinkle with parsley and serve immediately.

Mushroom vol-au-vents

Of all vol-au-vent fillings, mushrooms are my favourite. This makes 18–24 vol-au-vents. Use ready-made vol-au-vent cases which can be cooked frozen.

Filling

225 g (8 oz) chestnut or white buttons, wiped clean	2 cloves of garlic, peeled and chopped
12 g (½ oz) reconstituted dried ceps and their strained soaking liquid	280 ml (½ pint) ale
	salt
50 g (2 oz) butter	freshly milled black pepper
1 small onion, peeled and chopped	pinch of dried thyme
	4 tbs double cream
1 packet of frozen vol-au-vent cases	milk or beaten egg

Dice the mushrooms. Melt the butter in a heavy pan. Soften the onion over a medium heat, stirring well. Add the diced mushrooms and the ceps and fry them gently for 3–4 minutes. Add the garlic and mix well. Pour in the soaking liquid and the ale. Season and add the thyme. Raise the heat and boil the mixture dry. Add the cream and heat it through. Remove the mixture from the heat and reserve the filling. Preheat the oven to 220°C/425°F/gas mark 7.

Arrange the vol-au-vent cases on a large, greased baking tray. Brush their rims with milk or beaten egg. Bake for 13–15 minutes or until they rise and the edges are golden. Fill them with the mushroom mixture. Cool them on a rack. (If you want to serve them hot, remove the cases from the oven as soon as they have risen, fill them with the mushroom mixture and return to the oven to heat through.)

Mushroom 'caviar'

Both recipes are very good spread on buttered rye bread. The first version is made with minced raw mushrooms that 'cook' in the onion and lemon juices, an idea based on one of Lesley Chamberlain's recipes in *The Food and Cooking of Russia* (Penguin). The second, more conventional one uses sautéed mushrooms that are subsequently chopped very finely. Both also make a very good canapés served in bite-sized portions, or a cold filling for cooked vol-au-vent cases. They make enough for six people.

Raw mushroom caviar

450 g (1 lb) white or chestnut buttons	2 cloves of garlic, peeled and finely chopped
1 large onion, peeled	salt
juice of a lemon	freshly milled black pepper

pinch of cayenne pepper
4 tbs sunflower oil
4 tbs soured cream or crème
    fraîche

3–4 fronds of fresh dill,
    washed and chopped

Wipe the mushrooms clean. Chop them as finely as you can. Process the onion in a food processor until reduced to a pulp. Scoop it out and strain the juice through a wire sieve, pressing the pulp with the back of a spoon to extract as much juice as possible.

Transfer the mushrooms to a large bowl and combine them with the onion and lemon juices, chopped garlic and seasoning. Cover them with a plate, weigh it down with a heavy object and set aside for several hours. Drain away the liquid that will have collected in the bowl. Mix in the remaining ingredients and refrigerate. (The flavours will improve overnight.)

Cooked mushroom caviar

4 tbs sunflower oil
1 medium onion, peeled and
    chopped
2 cloves of garlic, peeled and
    chopped
450 g (1 lb) white or
    chestnut buttons, chopped

1–2 tbs white wine vinegar
    or cider vinegar
salt
freshly milled black pepper
handful of fresh parsley,
    washed and chopped

Heat the oil in a large frying pan and fry the onion and garlic until soft and lightly coloured. Add the mushrooms and fry for about 5 minutes, initially over a high heat, then more gently. Stir in the vinegar and cook gently for 3 more minutes. Season and mix in the parsley. Allow the mushrooms to cool, then mince them on a chopping board. Serve at room temperature.

Horse mushroom bruschette

Horse mushrooms can be very abundant in a good year and have the additional virtue of appearing in summer, when few other wild mushrooms are around. They are an excellent edible species with a deeply mushroomy taste and a hint of anise. Mature specimens can be enormous (but make sure they are still firm and free of maggots, whose presence is betrayed by little holes on the stem and caps). The chocolate-coloured gills of all but the youngest specimens (which have greyish-white gills) give a characteristic dark colour to this dish. Alternatively, see the recipe following this one for mushroom bruschette, which uses cultivated mushrooms. Enough for four people.

crusty bread
225 g (8 oz) horse
   mushrooms (caps only)
50 g (2 oz) unsalted butter
salt
freshly milled black pepper

clove of garlic, peeled and
   chopped
handful of fresh parsley,
   washed and chopped
6–8 tbs extra virgin olive oil

Cut 6–8 fairly thick slices of bread. Wipe the horse mushrooms clean and slice them. Melt the butter in a non-stick frying pan. Add the mushrooms and stir-fry over a high heat for a minute or so, then reduce the heat and gently fry for about 5 minutes, turning the mushrooms from time to time. Season and add the garlic and parsley. Mix and continue to cook for a couple of minutes longer. Remove from the heat and allow the mushrooms to cool. While the mushrooms cool, preheat the grill. Lightly toast one side of each slice of bread.

Mince the mushrooms on a chopping board, using a cleaver or large knife. (Ensure that they are reduced to a coarse paste.) Re-heat the grill. Spread the mushroom mixture on the untoasted side of the bread slices. Drizzle about a tablespoon of extra virgin olive oil over each, place them under the grill, and allow the edges of the bread to turn golden-brown. Serve hot.

Mushroom bruschette

This recipe can be made with wild mushrooms, or with a combination of dried ceps and cultivated mushrooms. It is a delicious canapé and an impressive antipasto or first course. (If using dried ceps, soak 25 g (1 oz) in warm water for 20 minutes, strain the liquid through kitchen paper and reserve it, adding the mushrooms and their liquid at the same time as the wine.) Makes enough for six people.

4 tbs extra virgin olive oil
450 g (1 lb) fresh
   mushrooms, trimmed and
   sliced
3 slices of smoked bacon,
   trimmed and finely diced
2 cloves of garlic, peeled and
   chopped
salt
freshly milled black pepper

2 tbs tomato passata or 2
   canned plum tomatoes,
   chopped
110 ml (4 fl oz) white wine
generous handful of fresh
   parsley, chopped
1 ciabatta loaf (or a French
   baguette), sliced
extra virgin olive oil, to dress
   the bruschette

Heat the olive oil in a heavy pan and add the mushrooms and bacon. Sear them over a high heat, then reduce the heat and sauté for

3–4 minutes. Add the garlic and continue to sauté for another 3 minutes. Season, mix well and add the tomato and the wine. Reduce until the liquid has all but evaporated, and add the parsley. Stir and remove from the heat.

Preheat the grill; meanwhile, mince the mushroom mixture with two sharp knives or cleavers. Lightly toast the bread on one side, then spread the mushroom mixture thickly on the untoasted side. Pour over a trickle of olive oil and heat under the grill for 3–4 minutes. Serve hot.

Marinated button mushrooms

Choose small, crisp buttons that will retain some firmness while absorbing the rich flavour of the marinade ingredients, improving with time. Larger mushrooms can be halved or quartered. Serves four with other tapas, two as an appetizer.

2 tbs extra virgin olive oil	freshly milled black pepper
1 small onion, peeled and	pinch of oregano
very finely chopped	bay leaf
2 cloves of garlic, peeled and	2 cloves
chopped	2 tsp paprika
1 tbs tomato purée	pinch of cayenne pepper
110 ml (4 fl oz) white wine	350 g (12 oz) button
splash of brandy	mushrooms
salt	

Heat the oil in a pan, simmer the onion until translucent, then add the garlic. Stir. Add the remaining ingredients except the mushrooms. Cover and simmer for 30 minutes. Add the mushrooms and simmer them, covered, for about 6 minutes. Allow them to cool, cover and leave to marinate for 12–24 hours.

Marinated mushrooms

A delicious tapa or appetizer that improves after a long period of marination. Ordinary button mushrooms can be used, but chestnut mushrooms are slightly better-flavoured. Saffron and sherry give the sauce a character that is subtly different from the preceding recipe. Serves two, or four with other dishes.

350 g (12 oz) chestnut
  mushrooms, wiped clean,
  halved or quartered
2 tbs extra virgin olive oil
4 tbs tomato passata
2 shallots, peeled and
  chopped
1 clove of garlic, peeled and
  chopped

1 tbs wine vinegar
2 tbs dry sherry
salt
freshly milled black pepper
1 bay leaf
small piece of cinnamon bark
pinch of saffron strands
handful of fresh parsley,
  chopped

Combine all the ingredients except the parsley in a small saucepan. Bring to a simmer and cook, covered, for 15 minutes. Sprinkle with the parsley, remove from the heat and allow to cool. Leave to marinate for at least 6 hours, preferably a day.

Serve with bread and a selection of other appetizers not in sauce.

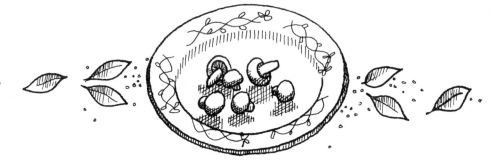

Champignons à la grecque

Other vegetables can be marinated in this fashion, but mushrooms are most delicious of all. Serves four with a selection of appetizers as long as they are not in a sauce. Charcuterie, pickles, and seafood are all good accompaniments.

400 g (14 oz) firm button
  mushrooms
6 tbs olive oil
110 ml (4 fl oz) white wine
1 tbs red wine vinegar
2 tbs tomato purée

1 tsp black peppercorns,
  lightly crushed
1 tsp coriander seeds
bay leaf
1 tsp salt

Wipe the mushrooms clean but leave them whole. Transfer them to a pan with the remaining ingredients. Bring to the boil, reduce the heat, and simmer for 25 minutes; the sauce should now be thick. Transfer to a covered serving bowl and refrigerate. Serve cold. The flavour improves after several hours.

BRUNCHES, FIRST COURSES AND LIGHT MEALS

Potatoes and mushrooms with paprika

Mushrooms and potatoes go very well together. In Spanish recipes such as this one, wild mushrooms would normally be used but cultivated mushrooms may be substituted. Serves four, accompanied by a green salad.

675 g (1½ lb) red potatoes
25 g (1 oz) butter
6 tbs olive oil
2 bay leaves
1 onion, peeled and chopped
2 cloves of garlic, peeled and
    chopped
350 g (12 oz) mushrooms,
    cleaned and thickly sliced
salt

freshly milled black pepper
pinch of grated nutmeg
1 tsp hot paprika or 1 tsp
    sweet paprika and a pinch
    of cayenne pepper
2 canned plum tomatoes,
    chopped
splash of white wine
handful of fresh parsley,
    washed and chopped

Peel the potatoes and cut them into small, even chunks. Heat the butter in a pan with the olive oil. Add the potatoes and bay leaves and stir-fry them for about 5 minutes, until evenly golden. Add the onion and garlic, mix well and sauté gently for 2 minutes. Add the mushrooms and mix well. Sauté the mushrooms for 5 more minutes, initially over a high heat, then more gently. Season with salt, pepper and a light grating of nutmeg, add the paprika and cayenne pepper (if using) and mix well. Add the tomatoes and a splash of wine. Mix again and cook for a minute or so. Mix in the parsley and serve.

Mushroom and potato gratin

Serve this delicious gratin as an appetizer or as a complete light lunch or supper for four, accompanied by a salad.

a little oil
225 g (8 oz) each of celeriac
  and waxy potatoes
225 g (8 oz) button
  mushrooms, stems
  trimmed
4 tbs olive oil, plus a little
  more for dressing the
  gratin
1 medium onion, peeled and
  chopped

4 cloves of garlic, peeled and
  chopped
generous handful of fresh
  parsley, washed and
  chopped
salt
freshly milled black pepper
225 ml (8 fl oz) white wine
175 g (6 oz) grated mature
  cheddar or gruyère cheese

Lightly oil a deep-sided oven dish. Preheat the oven to 200°C/400°F/gas mark 6.

Peel and slice the celeriac and potatoes very thinly. Slice the mushrooms.

Heat 4 tbs of olive oil in a frying pan and add the onion and mushrooms. Sauté over a high heat for 5–6 minutes, add half the chopped garlic and the parsley, and season. Add half of the wine and boil it off, stirring well. Spoon a thin layer of the mixture into the bottom of the oven dish.

Mix the roots together and arrange half of them over the mushroom layer, overlapping slightly. Sprinkle with a little garlic, moisten with wine and a few drops of olive oil and top with some of the grated cheese. Season lightly. Repeat the process, reserving some cheese to finish. Bake for 35 minutes or until soft and golden.

Braised mushrooms with beans

Mushrooms and beans are excellent partners. This is a warming dish that may be made with fresh wild mushrooms, or with the trusty combination of cultivated mushrooms and reconstituted dried ceps; both versions are very good indeed. Serves four with fried polenta squares or crusty bread.

350 g (12 oz) firm wild
  mushrooms, cleaned or
350 g (12 oz) cultivated
  mushrooms and
12 g (½ oz) reconstituted

dried ceps and their strained
  soaking liquid
4 tbs extra virgin olive oil
1 medium onion, peeled and
  chopped

1 stick celery, thinly sliced
2 cloves of garlic, peeled and
  chopped
400 g (14 oz) canned borlotti
  or cannellini beans, drained
handful of fresh parsley,
  washed and chopped

200 g (7 oz) canned plum
  tomatoes, chopped
6 tbs dry white wine
salt
freshly milled black pepper

Slice the fresh mushrooms, or leave them whole if they are small. Heat the oil in a pan with the onion, celery and garlic. Sweat the vegetables for about 5 minutes, to soften them. Add the mushrooms and stir-fry them gently with the vegetables for 8 more minutes. Add the ceps' soaking liquid (if using), raise the heat and allow it to boil away. Add the beans, parsley, tomatoes, and wine. Reduce the heat, season well and cover. Simmer for about 20 minutes. Serve.

Mushroom and flageolet bean stew

A hearty and warming stew to enjoy on cold nights. The herbs and red wine give the stew a subtly different character from that of the preceding recipe. Serves two.

4 tbs olive oil
sprig of thyme
sprig of sage
2 large open-cap mushrooms,
  stems trimmed and thickly
  sliced
6 shiitake mushrooms, stems
  trimmed and thickly sliced
12 g (½ oz) reconstituted
  dried ceps and their
  soaking liquid

3 cloves of garlic, peeled and
  chopped
glass of red wine
4 tinned plum tomatoes,
  chopped
425 g (15 oz) can of flageolet
  beans, rinsed and drained
salt
freshly milled black pepper

Heat the oil in a pan and simmer the thyme and sage leaves. Add all the mushrooms and garlic, increase the heat and fry for 5 minutes. Add the wine, tomatoes, beans, and the ceps' soaking liquid. Season. Cover and simmer for 15 minutes. Serve with fried polenta or crusty bread.

Braised saffron milk caps

Saffron milk caps (so called because the gills bleed a saffron-coloured milk when cut) can be quite plentiful in the autumn. They are valued chiefly for their excellent, firm texture which withstands cooking. Here they are lightly braised in a rich sauce. Other firm-textured wild mushrooms can be substituted, as can cultivated chestnut mushrooms. Eat with crusty bread or pasta. Serves four.

350 g (12 oz) saffron milk caps	salt
3 tbs olive oil	freshly milled black pepper
2 slices smoked bacon, trimmed and diced small	4 tbs white wine
1 small onion, peeled and chopped	4 tbs tomato passata
1 clove of garlic, peeled and finely chopped	2 tbs double cream
	small bunch of fresh chives, washed and chopped

Clean the mushrooms. Remove and discard the stems, and cut the caps into thick slices.

Heat the olive oil. Fry the bacon; before it browns, add the mushrooms and onion. Stir-fry over a high heat for 2–3 minutes. Reduce the heat, add the garlic, mix well, and gently fry for 2–3 minutes longer. Season and add the wine and tomatoes. Cook over a medium heat until the sauce thickens (this will just take 3–4 minutes). Mix in the cream, heat through, sprinkle with chives, and serve.

Grilled mushrooms

Ceps with large but firm caps are the ideal mushrooms to grill but others with firm caps, including open-cap cultivated mushrooms, may be substituted. Serve one large or two smaller caps per person.

4–8 large, firm mushrooms, wiped clean	4 generous handfuls of fresh parsley, washed and chopped
4 cloves of garlic, peeled and finely chopped	extra virgin olive oil
2 shallots, peeled and very finely chopped	salt
	freshly milled black pepper

Preheat the grill. Chop the mushrooms' trimmed stems finely and mix them with the garlic, shallots and parsley. Arrange the mushroom caps on a clean baking pan, the stem sides facing up. Drizzle olive oil liberally over the mushrooms and season them with salt and pepper. Grill for about 3 minutes, then invert the mushrooms, pour a little more oil over the caps, and season. Grill for 4 minutes. Invert the mushrooms again so that the stem sides face up. Spoon the parsley mixture into the cavities and drizzle more oil over them; grill for 2–3 minutes, spoon some of the pan juices over the mushrooms and serve hot with crusty bread.

Cèpes à la Bordelaise

This is the traditional way of cooking wonderful firm, young ceps in the Bordeaux area. A common variation is the addition of breadcrumbs. You can substitute whole cultivated button mushrooms, although the taste will be less intense. Serves four as a starter.

675 g (1½ lbs) firm ceps or closed-cap chestnut mushrooms
140 ml (5 fl oz) olive oil
4 cloves of garlic, peeled and chopped

salt
freshly milled black pepper
2 handfuls of fresh parsley, washed and chopped
juice of ½ a lemon or 4 tbs dry white wine

If you are fortunate enough to have bought or gathered young wild ceps, use a very sharp knife to shave away any hard, soiled bottoms. Clean them by brushing or scraping away any dirt and leave whole, if they are very small, or slice them thickly. If using cultivated mushrooms, leave them whole if they are tight buttons, or halve them.

Heat the oil in a seasoned frying pan and put in the mushrooms. Sear them over a high heat for a minute or two, then reduce the heat and after about 4 minutes add the garlic. Stir well and season. Continue to sauté for 4 minutes, then add the parsley, and lemon juice or wine. Increase the heat to reduce the liquid, which will only take a minute. Serve in warmed individual terracotta ramekins, with a salad and crusty bread.

Morilles à la creme

This is one of the finest – and simplest – mushroom recipes I know. It is well worth taking the trouble to buy fresh morels in their short spring season. Alternatively, use fresh cultivated mushrooms and some reconstituted dried morels. The health-conscious can substitute unsweetened fromage frais for the cream. Serves two with toasted or lightly baked brioches or on fried bread.

225 g (8 oz) fresh morels or
   175 g (6 oz) cultivated
   mushrooms and
   18 g (⅔ oz) dried morels
25 g (1 oz) butter
2 shallots, peeled and finely
   chopped
1 clove of garlic, peeled and
   finely chopped

salt
freshly milled black pepper
pinch of grated nutmeg
handful of fresh parsley,
   washed and chopped
3–4 tbs double cream or
   fromage frais

Wash the fresh morels thoroughly to remove all traces of grit. Drain them well or shake them dry. Slice each one in half, from top to bottom.

If using cultivated mushrooms, wipe them clean and trim off the bottoms of the stems. Slice the mushrooms. Soak the dried morels for 30 minutes in a cup of hot water. Remove them; strain and reserve their soaking liquid.

Melt the butter in a pan with the mushrooms. Stir-fry them over a high heat for 2–3 minutes, then reduce the heat and sauté them for about 2 minutes longer. Add the shallots and garlic. Mix, raise the heat and stir-fry for about 3 minutes longer. (Add the soaking liquid now and allow it to boil away.) Season with salt, pepper and nutmeg and throw in the parsley. Mix well and add the cream. Cook for less than a minute, to heat and thicken the cream. Serve at once.

Mushroom quiche

In Alsace, shortcrust pastry quiches (from *kuchen*, the German word for cake) are filled with a custard made with eggs and cream, to which various other savoury ingredients such as onions, bacon or ham, tomatoes, and, best of all, mushrooms are added. I like to include grated parmesan cheese in the custard, although, strictly speaking, the ingredient is alien to Alsace. Try the recipe with fresh wild mushrooms; alternatively, use a combination of dried ceps and cultivated mushrooms (or even just the latter). Serves four.

oil
flour
225 g (8 oz) shortcrust
   pastry (thawed, if frozen)
baking beans
2 tbs olive oil or porcini oil
   (see recipe on p. 111)
40 g (1½ oz) butter
4 shallots, peeled and chopped

1 clove of garlic, peeled and
   finely chopped
225 g (8 oz) mushrooms,
   sliced
12 g (½ oz) reconstituted
   dried ceps and their
   strained soaking liquid
   (optional)
salt

freshly milled black pepper
handful of fresh parsley,
    washed and chopped
3 eggs, beaten
140 ml (5 fl oz) single cream

40 g (1½ oz) piece of
    parmesan, freshly grated
½ tsp salt
leaves from 3 sprigs fresh
    tarragon, washed

Preheat the oven to 220°C/425°F/gas mark 7. Lightly oil a 23 cm (9 inch) flan tin. Apply a little flour to a clean work surface and roll out the ball of pastry to a disc that just overlaps the tin. Line the tin with the pastry and trim off any jagged edges. Prick the pastry base repeatedly with a fork. Line the pastry with a sheet of greaseproof paper, and weigh down with baking beans. Bake blind for 10 minutes. Remove the paper and the baking beans. Ensure that the base is almost dry and lightly coloured; if still soggy, return it to the oven for a few minutes longer.

Now make the filling. Heat the olive or porcini oil in a pan with the butter. Add the shallots and fry them gently for a few minutes, to soften them. Add the garlic, mix well, and add the mushrooms (and reconstituted ceps, if using). Stir-fry over a high heat for 2 minutes, then reduce the heat and cook for 2–3 minutes longer. Season, add the parsley, and mix well. If using dried ceps pour in the strained soaking liquid now; boil it off over a medium-high heat, which will take just a few minutes. Cover the base of the pastry with the mushroom mixture.

Beat the eggs with the cream and parmesan and season with salt. Pour the mixture over the mushrooms, ensuring that it does not spill over the sides. Scatter over the tarragon leaves and bake at 180°C/350°F/gas mark 4 for 35–40 minutes, by which time the surface will have set and browned a little. Serve at any temperature with a salad.

Horn of plenty brioches

These elegant black or dark-grey members of the chanterelle family are among the most highly prized wild mushrooms, and need only simple preparation. Here, they are cooked very simply in cream and served with toasted brioche bread which can be bought ready-made in supermarkets. Common chanterelles or winter chanterelles are equally suitable, or substitute shiitake and oyster mushrooms.

4 brioches	salt
50 g (2 oz) unsalted butter	freshly milled black pepper
400 g (14 oz) mushrooms,	225 ml (8 fl oz) single cream
cleaned	handful of fresh parsley,
2 cloves of garlic, peeled and	washed and chopped
finely chopped	

Slice the brioches open horizontally. Make shallow hollows by removing some of the soft centres.

Melt the butter in a pan and add the mushrooms. Stirring often, gently fry them until they are tender (about 8 minutes), then add the garlic. Mix well, season, and continue to fry gently over a medium heat for about 3 more minutes. Add the cream and the parsley, mix well, and heat through. Reserve. Lightly toast the brioches on both sides. Meanwhile, reheat the mushroom mixture briefly. Fill the hollows with the mushroom mixture. Serve at once with a green salad.

St George's parcels

These filo parcels are named after the fleshy, perfumed mushroom which appears around St George's Day (23 April). An equally delicious version can be prepared in late autumn with richly scented wood or field blewits. At all other times, a combination of fresh cultivated mushrooms and dried and reconstituted morels or ceps may be substituted, although the flavour will be quite different. Serves four.

4 tbs olive oil
1 medium onion, peeled and
   finely chopped
225 g (8 oz) St George's
   mushrooms, cleaned and
   chopped
110 g (4 oz) fresh morels,
   cleaned and chopped
pinch of dried thyme

2 cloves of garlic, peeled and
   finely chopped
salt
freshly milled black pepper
140 ml (5 fl oz) single cream
350 g (12 oz) frozen filo
   pastry, thawed
olive oil for oiling the pastry
milk

Heat the olive oil in a frying pan and sauté the onion over a medium heat for 2 minutes. Add the mushrooms and sauté for 6 minutes. Add the thyme and garlic and sauté for 2 more minutes. Season, add the cream, lower the heat, and simmer for 4–5 minutes to reduce the sauce. Remove from the heat.

Preheat the oven to 220°C/425°F/gas mark 7. Lightly oil an oven dish. Carefully separate the filo leaves and brush each one with oil. Divide the sheets into four neat stacks. Cut each stack in half lengthways. Pile the mushroom mixture at one end of each of the eight strips. Fold them over and over, to make parcels. Brush with milk and bake until golden-brown. Serve at once with a green salad.

Wild mushroom pillows

Ready-made puff pastry can be used to make these 'pillows'. I generally use a mixture of wild mushrooms. Alternatively, use a combination of 12 g (½ oz) of dried ceps and cultivated mushrooms. This makes an appetizing first course for four, or light meal for two, accompanied by a salad.

225 g (8 oz) puff pastry
   (thawed, if frozen)
flour
3 tbs olive oil
400 g (14 oz) wild
   mushrooms, cleaned,
   trimmed and sliced, or
   400 g (14 oz) cultivated
   mushrooms and
   12 g (½ oz) reconstituted
   dried ceps with their
   strained soaking liquid

pinch of dried thyme (or 3
   fresh sprigs)
salt
freshly milled black pepper
2 tsp brandy
2 cloves of garlic, peeled and
   finely chopped
1 egg, beaten, or milk

Preheat the oven to 220°C/425°F/gas mark 7.

Roll out the puff pastry on a floured work surface (apply flour to the rolling pin, too), and cut out 16 sheets, each 4 cm (2 inches) square.

Heat the olive oil in a pan and add the mushrooms and the thyme. Stir-fry them over a medium heat until their bulk has reduced by approximately a third (about 4 minutes). If using dried ceps, add the soaking liquid now and allow it to evaporate. Season, add the brandy and garlic, mix well and continue to fry gently over a low heat for 5 more minutes, stirring occasionally. Transfer to a clean chopping surface and mince the mushroom mixture roughly.

Spoon the mixture into the centre of half of the sheets. Cover with the remaining sheets and pinch the edges together, folding them over and moistening the edges, to seal. You should have plump pillows.

Transfer the pillows to lightly oiled oven dishes, paint the upper surfaces and the folds with the beaten egg or milk and bake until they are an appetizing golden-brown (about 15 minutes).

Oyster mushroom puffs

Serve these puffs as an elegant but easy and relatively quick first course. Wild oyster mushrooms have excellent flavour, but almost any mushrooms can be substituted. This recipe serves four as an appetizer, or two as a satisfying lunch or supper.

flour	*salt*
250 g (8 oz) puff pastry	*freshly milled black pepper*
(thawed, if frozen)	*2 canned plum tomatoes,*
1 egg, beaten	*chopped*
2 tbs olive oil	*1 tbs concentrated crème*
250 g (8 oz) oyster	*fraîche*
mushrooms, sliced	*fresh parsley, washed and*
2 cloves of garlic, peeled and	*finely chopped*
finely chopped	

Preheat the oven to 220°C/425°F/gas mark 7. Ensure that the pastry is at room temperature.

Apply a little flour to a work surface and the surface of a rolling pin. Cut the puff pastry into four equal sections; roll them into circles (do not roll out too thinly). Pinch up the edges with your thumb and forefinger to make rims. Transfer to a lightly oiled oven dish, paint the surfaces with the beaten egg and bake until the pastry has risen and is coloured golden brown, about 15 minutes.

While the puffs are baking, prepare the mushroom topping. Heat the olive oil and add the mushrooms. Stir them over a high heat for 2 minutes, then reduce to medium and gently fry for 4 more minutes. Add the garlic, season well and continue to fry gently for another minute or so. Add the plum tomatoes, mix well and cook for about

5 minutes. Add the crème fraîche and heat through. Divide the mushroom mixture into four portions and spoon onto the four puffs. Sprinkle with the parsley and serve with a salad.

Mushroom pierogi

These little Russian pies can be made quickly with packet puff pastry, with excellent results. When they are in season, I use mixed wild mushrooms, moistened with a little beer, instead of the dried mushrooms' soaking liquid; either way, allow the liquid to boil away before adding the soured cream. This makes a dozen *pierogi*.

12 g (½ oz) reconstituted
  dried ceps and their
  strained soaking liquid
25 g (1 oz) butter
1 tbs vegetable oil
3 shallots, peeled and
  chopped
225 g (8 oz) mushrooms,
  chopped

salt
freshly milled black pepper
fresh parsley or dill, washed
  and chopped
3 tbs soured cream
500 g (18 oz) packet of puff
  pastry (thawed if frozen)
milk or beaten egg

Chop the ceps. Heat the butter and oil in a frying pan. Add the shallots and the fresh and dried mushrooms, raise the heat and stir-fry for 2 minutes over a high heat. Reduce the heat and cook very gently for 10 minutes, stirring occasionally. Raise the heat to maximum, add the ceps' soaking liquid (or a glass of beer) and allow it to boil away. Season and add the parsley or dill, mixing well. Add the soured cream and cook for a minute until the mixture has thickened. Reserve the mushrooms. Preheat the oven to 200°C/400°F/gas mark 6.

Shape the pastry into a ball. On a floured work surface, roll it out into a thin disc. Stamp out about two dozen circles, 8 cm (3 in) in diameter, with an inverted tumbler or large wine glass. Transfer half of the pastry discs to oiled baking trays. Spoon a little of the mushroom mixture into the centres of the discs (do not overfill them). Cover with the remaining pastry circles, moisten the edges and press them together with the tines of a fork. Brush the surfaces with milk or beaten egg. Bake for 15–20 minutes or until golden. Serve hot.

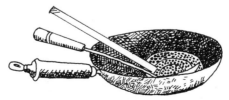

Mushroom gulyas

Hungarians cook many different ingredients in paprika, not least wild mushrooms, for which they share a passion with other central Europeans. I saw Anton Mosimann cook a simple mushroom gulyas on a television programme shot in Hungary and decided to experiment, adding a little wine and soured cream and substituting fresh dill for chopped celery leaf. This is the resulting recipe which may be served with rice, potatoes or noodles, or just with lightly baked and buttered slices of brioche bread. Use a mixture of wild or cultivated mushrooms, cut into quite thick slices, or left whole if they are small or delicate. Serves two as a light lunch or supper, or four as a starter.

4 tbs olive oil
110 g (4 oz) shallots, peeled
* and chopped*
2 cloves of garlic, peeled and
* finely chopped*
400 g (14 oz) very fresh
* mushrooms, cleaned*
salt
1 tbs hot paprika or 1 tbs
* sweet paprika and a pinch*
* of cayenne pepper*

1 tbs tomato passata
3 tbs white wine
110 ml (4 fl oz) soured
* cream*
2 fronds of fresh dill, washed
* and chopped*

Heat the olive oil and sweat the shallots until they are soft. Add the garlic, stir, and add the mushrooms. Raise the heat and cook for 4–5 minutes, stirring often. Season with salt and paprika, and stir. Add the tomato and wine and simmer for 3 minutes or until the liquid has thickened. Add the soured cream and heat through. Sprinkle with dill and serve.

Gourmet mushrooms on toast

In the first version, ordinary button mushrooms are enriched with cream and spiced with fino sherry. In the second, they are flavoured with brandy and smoked bacon. The third calls for wild horse mushrooms which are so delicious as to need very little in the way of culinary embellishment. All are very tasty and elevate mushrooms on toast to a higher gastronomic level. Each recipe serves four.

Version 1

50 g (2 oz) unsalted butter
575 g (1¼ lb) crisp button
   mushrooms, sliced
salt
freshly milled black pepper

5 tbs dry sherry
110 ml (4 fl oz) single cream
generous bunch of chives,
   snipped

Melt the butter in a heavy pan. Add the mushrooms and gently fry them over a medium heat until they have browned slightly (about 6 minutes), stirring from time to time. Season the mushrooms, pour in the sherry, and allow it to reduce (this will just take a few seconds); pour in the cream. Allow the sauce to thicken a little, sprinkle with the chives, and divide into four equal portions. Serve at once on hot toast.

Version 2

3 tbs olive oil
4 slices smoked bacon,
   trimmed of fat and diced
575 g (1¼ lb) flat or open
   cup mushrooms, sliced
2 cloves of garlic, peeled and
   finely chopped

salt
freshly milled black pepper
2 tbs brandy
handful of fresh parsley,
   chopped

Heat the oil in a well-seasoned or non-stick frying pan. Fry the bacon, and before it turns crisp, add the mushrooms. Mix well, reduce the heat to medium, and gently fry for about 5 minutes. Add the garlic, mix well, season, and fry for 2–3 more minutes. Add the brandy and heat through. Sprinkle with parsley and serve on hot buttered toast.

Version 3

Clean 675 g (1½ lb) mushrooms and discard the stems. Slice the caps. Melt 75 g (3 oz) butter in a heavy pan. Add the mushrooms and fry for about 3 minutes, then reduce the heat and sauté for 5 more minutes. Season, add a handful of chopped parsley and mix. Serve on hot buttered toast.

Stuffed mushrooms

I have never grasped the point of Shirley Conran's famous aphorism in *Superwoman*, 'life is too short to stuff a mushroom', since stuffed mushrooms are quick and easy to prepare. All three methods given here are very good with open-cap cultivated mushrooms, although you could substitute wild field and horse mushrooms, parasol or shaggy parasol mushrooms. Each recipe serves two.

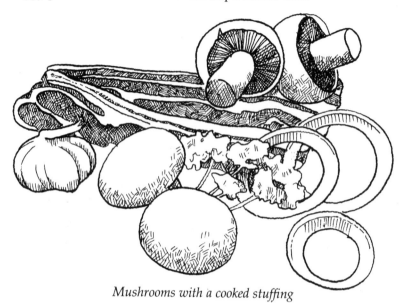

Mushrooms with a cooked stuffing

4 very large (but firm) mushroom caps, about 450 g (1 lb) (or 8 medium-sized ones)
110 ml (4 fl oz) extra virgin olive oil
3 slices of bacon or pancetta, trimmed and diced
half a medium onion, peeled and diced
2 ripe tomatoes, peeled and diced
2 cloves of garlic, peeled and finely chopped
splash of white wine
6 tbs fresh breadcrumbs
large handful of fresh parsley, washed and chopped
salt
freshly milled black pepper

Wipe the caps clean and set them aside. Preheat a grill. Heat 2 tbs of the olive oil in a small, non-stick or well-seasoned frying pan and fry the bacon until it just begins to colour. Add the onion and soften in the oil over a medium heat. Add the tomato and garlic, mix well, and cook for a few minutes. Moisten the pan with wine, let it evaporate, then remove the pan from the heat.

Combine the breadcrumbs and parsley with the cooked ingredients, season, and mix well. Drizzle half of the remaining olive oil onto the convex sides of the caps and grill them for 3–4 minutes. Turn, and spoon a mound of the mixture onto their concave sides, drizzle with the remaining oil and grill for 3–4 more minutes. Serve hot with a salad.

Mushrooms stuffed with blue cheese and ham

225 g (8 oz) blue cheese, at
 room temperature
2 tsp brandy
50 g (2 oz) cooked ham,
 finely diced
handful of fresh parsley,
 washed and chopped

4 very large, firm mushroom
 caps or 8 medium-sized
 ones (about 450 g (1 lb))
olive oil
salt
freshly milled black pepper
25 g (1 oz) butter, diced

Preheat the grill. Mash the cheese with the brandy, which will soften it. Work in the ham and parsley and continue to mash the mixture to a paste.

Wipe the mushrooms clean. Place them under the grill, convex sides up. Drizzle a little olive oil over them, and season. Grill them for 4 minutes. Turn, and spread the cheese mixture over their concave sides. Dot with butter, season, and grill for 3–4 more minutes. Serve hot, accompanied by a salad.

Baked mushrooms stuffed with pine nuts

175 g (6 oz) open-cap
 mushrooms
3 tbs olive oil
2 cloves of garlic, peeled and
 chopped
3 canned plum tomatoes,
 chopped
4 tbs dry white wine
salt

freshly milled black pepper
4 tbs pine nuts
generous handful of fresh
 parsley, washed and
 chopped
50 g (2 oz) parmesan,
 freshly grated
extra virgin olive oil

Preheat an oven to 200°C/400°F/gas mark 6. Wipe the mushroom caps clean. Heat the oil in a small pan. Add the garlic, tomatoes, white wine and seasoning, and cook over a medium heat for about 5 minutes, or until the sauce has thickened. Add the pine nuts and parsley and mix well. Stuff the mushrooms with the mixture, cover with parmesan and pour a thin trickle of olive oil over each. Bake until the parmesan has coloured (about 20 minutes) and serve hot with crusty bread.

Poached eggs with button mushrooms

The secret of poaching eggs perfectly is to add a little vinegar to the poaching water, which should simmer very gently. These quantities serve four people.

40 g (1½ oz) butter
450 g (1 lb) crisp button
mushrooms, sliced
salt
freshly milled black pepper
4 tbs dry sherry

110 ml (4 fl oz) single cream
generous bunch of chives,
snipped
4 slices buttered toast
1 tbs wine vinegar
4 free-range eggs

Melt the butter in a pan and gently fry the mushrooms over a medium heat, stirring from time to time, until they are golden (about 4–6 minutes). Season and moisten with the sherry. Add the cream, and remove from the heat when the sauce has thickened. Sprinkle with the chives.

Meanwhile, prepare buttered toast. Warm four plates.

Bring enough salted water to cover the eggs to a gentle simmer in a frying pan. Add the vinegar and carefully break each egg into the water, without breaking the yolks. (You may prefer to break each egg into a shallow cup or bowl first, then ease it in.) Poach the eggs until the yolks are covered in a thin opaque veil, spooning water over the domed yolks (or poach until done to the required degree of runniness). Lift them very carefully with a slotted spoon or spatula, drain thoroughly, and trim away any ragged white edges with a knife. Place them (on the buttered toast, if desired) in the centre of the plates. Reheat the mushrooms briefly, divide them equally into four portions and encircle the eggs with the mushrooms.

Scrambled eggs with chanterelles

A delightful, elegant and easy dish that goes well with chilled champagne and therefore is especially suitable for special occasions. Serves two.

40 g (1½ oz) unsalted
butter
175 g (6 oz) chanterelles,
cleaned but left whole
(unless large)
salt
freshly milled black pepper

generous handful of flat-
leaved parsley, washed and
chopped
5 large free-range eggs
pinch of salt
2–3 tbs single cream

Melt half of the butter in a small frying pan. Sauté the chanterelles over a medium-low heat for 6–8 minutes, stirring often. Season and mix in the parsley. Set aside while you scramble the eggs.

Beat the eggs lightly with a pinch of salt and the cream. Put the remaining butter into a non-stick or well-seasoned frying pan. Pour in the eggs, scrambling them with a fork over a medium heat. (Always scrape the eggs back towards the centre of the pan, and do not allow them to set completely.) Remove from the heat while still slightly moist, and divide into two equal portions. Quickly reheat the chanterelles. Pile the eggs onto hot buttered toast, covering them with the chanterelles.

Note: If chanterelles are not available, other mushrooms such as oyster mushrooms are an acceptable alternative. A little wine and garlic are added to boost the flavour. Clean 175 g (6 oz) mushrooms and slice any large ones. Proceed as in the previous recipe, but add a finely chopped clove of garlic and a splash of wine and allow the wine to evaporate.

Fairy ring omelettes

Fairy ring mushrooms are much appreciated in France, both fresh and dried, and many a country omelette is cooked with a delicate stuffing of *mousserons*. (Confusingly, this is also the name of the St George's mushroom, undoubtedly because they both share the same habitat and the fairy rings or half-rings of darker grass are also a clue pointing to the latter, which appears around St George's Day.) I enjoy picking fairy ring mushrooms when they first appear, after rain, in early summer. My favourite spot also provides an abundance of wild rocket, young dandelion leaves for an accompanying green salad, and masses of blackberries in the early autumn. You could substitute button mushrooms. This serves two.

25 g (1 oz) unsalted butter	2 tbs double cream
110 g (4 oz) fresh fairy caps	a little chopped fresh parsley
(stems removed), chopped	2 tsp olive oil
salt	6 eggs, lightly beaten
freshly milled black pepper	salt

Melt the butter and sauté the mushrooms over a medium heat for 2 minutes. Reduce the heat and gently stew them in the fat for 4–5 more minutes. Season them well, add the cream and parsley and keep warm.

Meanwhile, heat a small, well-seasoned or non-stick frying pan and add 1 tsp of olive oil. Swirl it around and as soon as it smokes, add half of the beaten egg mixture. Tip the pan to allow the eggs to run, add half of the mushroom mixture, and fold the omelette three ways, to enfold the filling. Quickly turn it, cook for a few seconds more, and turn onto a cold plate. Serve, and repeat the process.

Frittata di chiodini

Honey fungus is an abundant and virulent parasitic fungus that destroys trees. It happens also to be a good edible species. Unfortunately, honey fungus is not really suited to sauces, as it turns liquids unpleasantly gluey. However, the caps are very good simply blanched and then sautéed in olive oil, with garlic, salt and pepper and a little fresh parsley. (Cooking removes a certain mild toxicity in the raw fungus that becomes more pronounced in large older specimens, which therefore should always be avoided). Here, young honey fungus caps are simply cooked in a rustic omelette that is quite unlike the classic French version; whereas the latter is cooked rapidly, maintaining a runny centre, Italian omelettes are fried in olive oil or butter without stirring, and have a more solid consistency. Look for the immature mushrooms, with fleecy veils still attached to the stems. This recipe serves two hungry people, or the frittata may be quartered to make a tasty appetizer for four. You could make a frittata with cultivated mushrooms, omitting the blanching.

> 110 g (4 oz) honey fungus
>   caps
> 6 large free-range eggs
> 25 g (1 oz) freshly grated
>   parmesan
>
> 4 tbs extra virgin olive oil
> salt
> freshly milled black pepper

Blanch the mushrooms in boiling water for a minute or two. Discard the water and rinse them in fresh water. Pat them dry with paper towels.

Beat the eggs lightly with the parmesan. Heat the olive oil in a well-seasoned or non-stick frying pan. Stir-fry the mushrooms in the oil for a few minutes. Season well, and pour in the beaten eggs. 'Fry' the eggs in the oil, ensuring that the mushrooms are embedded in the eggs as they set. Place the pan under a hot grill before the surface has set completely and allow the omelette to rise a little and turn golden. Serve at once, halved or quartered. Crusty bread or french fries are equally good accompaniments, and the omelette may be served cold.

Frittata di porcini

A delicious Tuscan frittata for two people that is just as simple to prepare as the preceding one. Ideally calling for fresh ceps, it is equally delicious in the spring with fresh morels, or 12 g (½ oz) dried and reconstituted ceps or morels and some sliced chestnut mushrooms.

> *3 tbs extra virgin olive oil*
> *110 g (4 oz) fresh, sliced ceps or morels or 12 g (½ oz) reconstituted dried ceps or morels with their strained soaking liquid and 110 g (4 oz) sliced chestnut mushrooms*
>
> *salt*
> *freshly milled black pepper*
> *5 large free-range eggs*
> *12 g (½ oz) butter*
> *fresh parsley, chopped*

Clean, trim and slice the ceps thinly.

Heat the olive oil in a medium-sized, well-seasoned or non-stick frying pan. Over a high heat, fry the mushrooms for a couple of minutes, before reducing the heat and sautéeing them more gently for 4 more minutes, stirring occasionally. (Add the soaking liquid, if using, raise the heat and let it boil away). Season well and turn off the heat while you beat the eggs lightly with a pinch of salt. Preheat the grill. Add a knob of butter and reheat the pan, pour in the eggs, and mix in the parsley. 'Fry' the omelette, ensuring that the mushrooms and parsley are well embedded as the eggs set. Slip the pan under the grill to set the surface of the omelette which is ready when the crust is golden. Lift from the pan, halve or quarter the omelette and serve hot or cold, with crusty bread and a salad.

Gnocchi ai funghi

Gnocchi are an ancient food. Before potatoes were introduced from the New World they were made with semolina dough, and feature in Apicius' Roman cookery book. Today potato gnocchi are especially identified with the northern regions of Italy while semolina gnocchi are popular in the south. A popular misconception is that they are heavy. On the contrary: freshly made, they are light and delicious.

Floury potato varieties work best. With a little practice, shaping them correctly gets easier. This recipe can be made with wild mushrooms, or with a combination of cultivated varieties and reconstituted dried ceps. It is worth making up the full quantity of gnocchi, as they will keep in the fridge but they should be dusted with semolina flour to prevent them from sticking together. Alternatively, use any leftover to bake a *pasticcio di gnocchi* (see opposite). The quantities given here are for four people.

Gnocchi

675 g (1½ lb) floury potatoes, peeled	2 tbs olive oil
	½ tsp salt
4 tbs milk	450 g (1 lb) plain flour

Put the potatoes and plenty of water into a large pot and bring to a boil. Cover and boil the potatoes until they are cooked, about 20 minutes. Pour away the water, add the milk, olive oil and salt and quickly mash the potatoes with a hand masher until they are completely smooth.

Allow the mixture to cool a little, then combine it with most of the flour, kneading thoroughly with floured hands. The dough should be smooth and elastic. Apply a little flour to a work surface, break up the dough into smaller balls and roll each out into long snakes, about the width of your finger. Cut into 1½ cm (⅔ inch) cylinders; press each one gently against the curved prongs of a fork, to leave ribbed indentations. Dust with flour and reserve them.

Sauce

3 tbs extra virgin olive oil	4 chopped peeled plum tomatoes (fresh or canned)
4 shallots, peeled and chopped	salt
350g (12 oz) wild mushrooms or	freshly milled black pepper
350 g (12 oz) cultivated mushrooms and	a few fresh basil leaves, washed or handful of fresh
12 g (½ oz) reconstituted dried ceps and their strained soaking liquid	parsley, washed and chopped
	freshly grated parmesan

Heat the olive oil in a pan with the shallots. Sauté them until soft and add the mushrooms. Raise the heat for the first 2 or 3 minutes of cooking, stirring constantly, then reduce and continue to cook for a few minutes longer. (Add the mushroom's soaking liquid now, if using, and allow it to evaporate.) Add the tomatoes, season, and cook until the sauce has thickened (about 5 more minutes). Meanwhile, bring plenty of salted water to a rolling boil in a large pot. Drop in the gnocchi and fish them out with a slotted spoon as soon as they float to the surface. Transfer to a heated serving dish, combine thoroughly with the sauce and the fresh herbs, and serve with freshly grated parmesan cheese.

Pasticcio di gnocchi

To serve two people you will need about half of the quantity of the original gnocchi recipe; 110 ml (4 fl oz) tomato passata; 110 g (4 oz) button mushrooms, thinly sliced; 1 packet of mozzarella (preferably *di bufala*), diced; 75 g (3 oz) freshly grated parmesan cheese; salt and freshly milled black pepper. Preheat the oven to 220°C/425°F/gas mark 7. In a shallow, oiled oven dish about 25 cm (10 inches) in diameter, layer half of the gnocchi, passata, mushroom slices, mozzarella and parmesan. Season, then repeat the sequence. Bake in the oven until the top is lightly golden (20–25 minutes).

Wild mushroom gnocchi

This version of potato gnocchi incorporates dried wild mushrooms, and can be simply served in a creamy sauce made with fresh mushrooms, with additional parmesan cheese. Alternatively, serve with some fresh sage leaves and 2 cloves of crushed garlic, briefly simmered in butter with freshly milled black pepper and extra parmesan. Serves four.

You will need 25 g (1 oz) reconstituted dried ceps and their strained soaking liquid. Process the mushrooms with the soaking liquid in a food processor.

Follow the main gnocchi recipe on p. 42 up to the point of adding the milk and oil to the boiled, mashed potatoes; replace these liquids with the processed ceps and proceed with the recipe. The gnocchi will be stained brown and acquire the full flavour of wild mushrooms.

Mushroom sauce

3 tbs olive oil
350 g (12 oz) mushrooms,
  cleaned, trimmed and
  thinly sliced
salt
freshly milled black pepper
2 cloves of garlic, peeled and
  finely chopped

6 tbs single cream
handful of fresh parsley,
  washed and chopped
50 g (2 oz) freshly grated
  parmesan cheese

Heat the olive oil in a heavy pan. Sear the mushrooms briefly over a high heat, then reduce the heat and gently fry them for 5–6 minutes. Season, and add the garlic; mix and gently fry for a minute or two longer. Add the cream, heat through and mix in the parsley. Combine thoroughly with the cooked gnocchi and plenty of parmesan.

Polenta con funghi

Polenta is an excellent vehicle for stewed wild mushrooms; it can be served freshly made and steaming, or allowed to cool, then fried, baked or grilled. However you serve it, it is always quite superb, especially on cool autumn nights. I use whatever wild mushrooms I may have to hand. Alternatively, use mixed cultivated mushrooms and some dried and reconstituted ceps with their strained soaking liquid. This serves four to six people.

Polenta

salt	*50 g (2 oz) butter*
1700 ml (3 pints) water	*50 g (2 oz) freshly grated*
375 g (13 oz) packet of	*parmesan*
Italian quick-cook polenta	*freshly milled black pepper*
(sometimes labelled '5	*a little grated nutmeg*
minuti')	

Bring a large pot of salted water to the boil. Rain in the polenta with one hand, while you stir all the while with the other. Keep stirring while the polenta thickens and sputters; it is cooked when, after 5 minutes or so, it comes away from the sides of the pot. (It will take up to 25 minutes to cook if you do not use the quick-cooking variety.)

Add the remaining ingredients, mixing thoroughly. It can be served hot, while still a porridge, or poured onto a wooden board, levelled and allowed to set as it cools. It can then be sliced into square or oblong shapes and shallow-fried in very hot olive oil, baked or grilled.

Mushroom sauce

3 tbs olive oil	*4 tbs water or stock*
450 g (1 lb) wild or	*salt*
cultivated mushrooms,	*freshly milled black pepper*
cleaned and sliced (left	*generous handful of fresh*
whole if small)	*parsley, washed and*
2 cloves of garlic, peeled and	*chopped*
finely chopped	*freshly grated parmesan*
110 ml (4 fl oz) tomato	*(optional)*
passata	

Heat the olive oil in a pan. Stir-fry the mushrooms for a few minutes, or until they have reduced in bulk. Add the garlic and mix. Add the tomato and water or stock, and cook until the sauce has thickened but still retains a little liquid. Season and mix in the parsley. Serve on a steaming mound of seasoned polenta, or next to fried, baked or grilled polenta squares, adding a little parmesan if desired.

Pizza ai funghi

This can be made with fresh, sliced ceps, or with cultivated mushrooms. The thin dough crisps on baking and is an authentic version of the pizzas Italians eat. Small domestic ovens require large, rigid baking sheets or oven pans to accommodate the pizzas. The dough can be kneaded by hand or with a machine fitted with dough hooks. This makes four smallish pizzas. Don't slice the mushrooms too thinly or they will dry out in the oven.

Dough

½ packet of dried yeast	*350 g (12 oz) plain flour*
(about 1½ tsp)	*1 tsp salt*
225 ml (8 fl oz) hot water	*1 tbs olive oil*

Dissolve the yeast in the water (unnecessary if fast-action yeast is used). Mix the flour, salt and olive oil in a bowl. Gradually add the yeast mixture, kneading all the while by hand, or by machine. When the dough is smooth and elastic, transfer it to an oiled container, cover with a clean cloth and leave to rest somewhere warm for an hour, or until it has doubled in size. Dust your hands, a work surface and a rolling pin with flour. Divide the dough into two balls and divide each ball into two. Roll out the four dough balls into discs about 20–23 cm (8–9 inches) in diameter, turning the dough to ensure circular shapes.
Preheat the oven to 220°C/425°F/gas mark 7.

Topping

3 tbs olive oil	*300 g (11 oz) Italian*
350 g (12 oz) cleaned ceps or	*mozzarella, diced*
chestnut mushrooms,	*generous pinch of oregano*
thickly sliced	*salt*
110 ml (4 fl oz) tomato	*freshly milled black pepper*
passata	*olive oil*

Heat the olive oil in a small pan. Sauté the fungi until partly cooked (3–4 minutes). Lift and reserve them. Place the pizzas on two well-oiled baking sheets. Spread a quarter of the tomato thinly over each. Dot evenly with mozzarella. Divide the mushrooms between the four pizzas. Sprinkle with the oregano. Season well and drizzle a little olive oil over each pizza. Bake in the oven on two shelves for 15–20 minutes. Check the pizzas to ensure that the edges and base are firm and lightly browned – you may have to swap the trays half-way through to ensure that all four pizzas cook evenly.

La parmigiana di melanzane

Normally prepared just with aubergines, tomato, and mozzarella and parmesan cheeses, this classic Campanian dish derives its name from the last ingredient. I find that some sliced, lightly fried mushrooms improve its texture and flavour. Serves four as an appetizer, or two as a light lunch or supper, with crusty bread.

2 large or 4 small aubergines, washed	*2 cloves of garlic, peeled and chopped*
salt	*salt*
3 tbs extra virgin olive oil	*freshly milled black pepper*
400 g (14 oz) can of tomatoes, chopped	*flour to coat the aubergines*
4 tbs white wine	*olive oil for frying*

225 g (8 oz) chestnut and shiitake mushrooms, thickly sliced
large handful of fresh basil leaves, washed

175 g (6 oz) Italian mozzarella, diced
75 g (3 oz) of parmesan, grated

Remove the aubergines' caps. Slice the aubergines evenly from end to end; the slices should be about 8 mm (⅓ inch) thick. Sprinkle with salt and let them bleed for half an hour. (If using smaller aubergines, omit this step so long as they are very fresh and firm.)

Meanwhile, combine in a pot the extra virgin oil, tomatoes, wine and garlic. Season and cook over a medium heat for about 15 minutes or until the sauce has thickened. Preheat the oven to 200°C/400°F/gas mark 6.

Wash the aubergines in fresh running water and pat them dry with kitchen paper. Dip them in flour, to coat. Heat a generous layer of olive oil in a large non-stick frying pan. Fry the aubergines in batches, until golden-brown. Drain and transfer them to a plate lined with kitchen paper. When they have all been fried, discard the oil and add a fresh, less generous layer. Heat the oil and sear the mushrooms on both sides for a minute or so, then remove and drain them on kitchen paper.

Spread a layer of tomato sauce over the base of a wide, shallow oven dish. Scatter over a few torn basil leaves. Cover with a layer of fried aubergines. Dot with mozzarella, sprinkle with parmesan, and scatter over some fried mushrooms. Repeat until all the ingredients have been used up, finishing with the cheeses and a little tomato sauce.

Bake until the cheese has melted and coloured golden-brown (about 15 minutes). Carefully drain off any surplus fat, rest for 5–10 minutes and serve warm or very warm but not piping hot.

Risotto ai funghi

Risotto is one of the best ways to cook wild mushrooms, especially ceps which are a great favourite throughout northern and central Italy where the 'porcini' are so intensely flavoured as to require very few extra ingredients other than onion or garlic, butter and stock. This version compensates for our slightly inferior mushrooms by the addition of fresh herbs, a little tomato and some reconstituted dried ceps. Serves four to six people. Any leftover rice can be mixed with a little flour, shaped into golf balls or sausages, and shallow fried in olive oil until golden.

1700 ml (3 pints) home-
made chicken stock (see
recipe on p. 114)
40 g (1½ oz) butter
2 tbs olive oil
medium onion, peeled and
chopped
350 g (12 oz) cultivated
shiitake and oyster
mushrooms, cleaned and
sliced
1 clove of garlic, peeled and
chopped
17 g (⅔ oz) reconstituted
dried ceps and their
strained soaking liquid

3 tbs tomato passata or 2
canned plum tomatoes,
chopped
salt
freshly milled black pepper
450 g (1 lb) arborio rice
a few fresh basil leaves,
washed and torn into
pieces, or handful of fresh
parsley, washed and
chopped
75 g (3 oz) freshly grated
parmesan

Bring the stock to a simmer, turn off the heat and cover to keep it warm.

Heat the butter and olive oil in a large, heavy frying pan. Fry the onion until lightly coloured. Add all the mushrooms and stir-fry for 3–4 minutes, until they reduce slightly. Add the garlic and mix well. Pour in the ceps' soaking liquid and allow it to evaporate. Add the tomato, season, and mix well. Cook the mixture for a few minutes longer, then add the rice and mix well with the sauce for a minute to coat all the grains. Pour in a generous ladle of stock, stir and allow the rice to absorb virtually all the liquid. Repeat, stirring constantly, until all the stock has been exhausted and the rice is tender and no longer soupy. Check the seasoning. Mix in the fresh herbs and half of the parmesan and let the risotto rest for a minute or two. Serve with the remaining parmesan and good bread.

Mushroom and walnut risotto

Serve this delicious risotto as an appetizer for four people, or as a light lunch or supper for two. The success of the dish is its creamy texture, an inherent quality of the starchy rice grains that is enhanced by the crushed walnuts. Needless to say, home-made stock (see recipes on p. 114) is better than a stock cube.

12 walnuts
50 g (2 oz) butter
2 tbs olive oil
1 medium onion, peeled and
chopped

1 carrot, scrubbed and diced
small
350 g (12 oz) button
mushrooms, thinly sliced

2 cloves of garlic, peeled and
  finely chopped
3 tbs tomato passata
salt
freshly milled black pepper
275 g (10 oz) arborio rice

1 litre (1¾ pints) chicken or
  vegetable stock
fresh basil leaves
75 g (3 oz) piece of
  parmesan, freshly grated

Stand the walnuts upright on a firm work surface. Tap the pointed ends with a hammer to smash the shells, and prise out the kernels. Put them in a food bag or enfold in a clean cloth, and crush them with a hammer.

Heat the butter and olive oil in a large, well-seasoned frying pan. Sauté the onion with the carrot until the vegetables are soft and have coloured lightly (about 3 minutes). Add the mushrooms and garlic and stir-fry over a higher heat for 3–4 minutes. Add the crushed walnuts, mix well, and spoon in the tomato. Mix well and season. Stir in the rice and cook for a minute or two.

Add a little stock, and allow the rice almost to dry out before adding more stock. Continue to cook the rice in this way, scraping the bottom of the pan to prevent the rice from sticking and burning, until all the stock has been used up and the rice is tender and creamy, about 25 minutes. Mix in a small handful of freshly torn basil leaves and half of the parmesan. Serve with the remaining parmesan.

Mushroom fried rice

Based on the fried rice dishes of eastern China, this easy recipe requires cold, cooked long-grain rice. Serves four.

1 egg
salt
2 tsp plus 1 tbs peanut oil
75 g (3 oz) lean cooked ham,
  diced
2 cloves of garlic, peeled and
  finely chopped
1 fresh chilli, washed and
  sliced
175 g (6 oz) button
  mushrooms, sliced
4 spring onions, washed and
  sliced

1 large, ripe tomato, peeled
  and diced
salt
1 tbs Shaohsing wine or dry
  sherry
675 g (1½ lb) cooked long-
  grain rice
110 g (4 oz) frozen peas,
  thawed
2 tbs light soy sauce
½ tbs dark soy sauce

Beat the egg with a pinch of salt. Heat 2 tsp of peanut oil in a small non-stick pan and make a small omelette. Transfer it to a plate and slice the omelette into thin strips.

Heat the remaining oil in a wok. When it just starts to smoke add the ham, garlic, chilli, mushrooms and the white parts of the spring onion. Stir-fry for about 2 minutes and add the tomato. Stir-fry for 1 more minute, season and add the Shaohsing wine. Stir-fry for another minute, then tip in the rice, breaking up any lumps. Add the peas, mix well, and add the soy sauces. Heat through, turning the rice with the wok scoop. Decorate with the strips of omelette and the green spring onion slices and serve immediately.

Fried oriental noodles with oyster mushrooms

These fried noodles are deliciously tangy. They can be made with any oriental noodles, whether the fresh, oily kind that are sometimes available in Chinese shops, or the more common dried rice or egg noodles. The quantities below will serve two people as a complete meal, four as a starter.

150 g (5 oz) dried oriental noodles, or a 450 g (1 lb) packet of fresh egg noodles	1 tbs Thai fish sauce
2 tbs peanut oil	1 tbs soy sauce
6 red shallots, peeled and chopped	1 tbs sugar
4 cloves of garlic, peeled and chopped	1 egg, beaten
2 fresh chillies, washed, seeded and sliced	110 g (4 oz) bean sprouts
110 g (4 oz) oyster mushrooms, sliced (left whole if small)	juice of a lime, or half a lemon
	50 g (2 oz) roasted peanuts, crushed
	handful of fresh coriander, washed and chopped
	½ tsp cayenne pepper

If using dried noodles, reconstitute them according to the packet instructions. (Fresh noodles can go straight into the wok.) Heat the oil to smoking point in a wok. Add the shallots, garlic and fresh chillies. Stir-fry them for a few seconds. Add the mushrooms and stir-fry a minute or so longer. Add the fish and soy sauces and the sugar. Mix well. Stir in the beaten egg and add the noodles. Stir-fry them for a minute. Add half of the bean sprouts, mix, and transfer the noodles to a warm platter. Squeeze the citrus juice over the noodles, scatter over the peanuts and coriander, and sprinkle with cayenne pepper. Surround the noodles with the remaining bean sprouts and serve immediately.

Three-mushroom curry

Three kinds of mushroom are curried in Thai 'red' curry paste, and simmered in coconut milk. The curry paste can be bought ready made in oriental shops, or made at home (see the recipe below). Serves four with rice or noodles and another dish.

25 g (1 oz) dried shiitake
  mushrooms
110 g (4 oz) oyster
  mushrooms
110 g (4 oz) button
  mushrooms
2 fresh red chillies
3 tbs peanut oil
1 small red onion, peeled and
  finely chopped
4 cloves of garlic, peeled and
  thinly sliced

1 tbs 'red' curry paste
1 tbs light soy sauce
1 tbs Thai fish sauce
2 tsp sugar
½ tsp salt
grated peel and juice of half a
  lime
225 ml (8 fl oz) canned
  coconut milk
50 g (2 oz) bean sprouts
dozen fresh basil leaves

Soak the shiitake mushrooms in hot water for 30 minutes. Strain and reserve the soaking liquid. Remove and discard the tough stalks. Slice the caps as finely as possible. Chop the fresh mushrooms coarsely. Split the chillies from top to bottom and remove the seeds. Slice the chillies thinly.

Heat the oil in a wok to smoking point. Add the onion and garlic and stir-fry them for a minute. Quickly add the curry paste and mix well. Stir-fry for 30 seconds, then add the mushrooms. Stir-fry them for a minute, then add the soy and fish sauces, the sugar and salt. Stir, and add the lime peel and juice. Stir, and pour in the strained mushroom soaking liquid. Cook until the liquid has reduced by half and add the coconut milk. Reduce the heat slightly and simmer the mushrooms for 5 minutes, or until the curry has thickened and reduced in volume by one third. Mix in the bean sprouts and transfer to a warm serving bowl. Scatter with the chillies and the basil and serve.

'Red' curry paste

In a blender or mortar process or pound the following: 8–10 dried red chillies, 6–8 red shallots, 6 cloves of garlic, 1 cm (½ inch) knob of peeled fresh ginger or galangal, the trimmed flesh of 1 red pepper, 1 thinly sliced stick of lemon grass, 1 cm (½ inch) piece of shrimp paste, 1 tsp salt, 1 tsp sugar, 2 tbs peanut oil. Stir in 2 tbs more oil. Transfer the paste to a small jar, cover with a thin layer of additional oil, screw on the lid and keep in the refrigerator.

Oyster mushroom pilau

Wild Indian monsoon mushrooms and morels from Kashmir are traditionally cooked in delicious rice pilaus, although cultivated mushrooms are familiar in India. I have found that oyster mushrooms make an excellent pilau although, naturally, fresh or dried and reconstituted morels may be substituted. Serves four to six people with any Indian meat or poultry dish.

350 g (12 oz) basmati rice
3 tbs peanut or vegetable oil
1 onion, peeled and finely chopped
small piece of cinnamon
2–3 cloves
½ tsp garam masala (see recipe below)
large, ripe tomato, peeled and chopped

175 g (6 oz) oyster mushrooms, cleaned, trimmed and sliced
560 ml (1 pint) home-made vegetable stock (see recipe on p. 114)
pinch of salt
handful of fresh coriander, washed and chopped

Soak the rice in plenty of fresh water. Gently squeeze the grains to release the starch. Drain the rice in a wire sieve.

Heat the oil in a saucepan. Fry the onion and spices gently in the oil until soft and coloured. Add the tomato and fry a little longer. Add the mushrooms, raise the heat and stir-fry them for 2–3 minutes. Stir in the rice and coat well in the oil. Pour in the stock and season with salt. Mix thoroughly, bring to the boil, cover and simmer over a very low heat for 12 minutes. Gently fold in the coriander and serve after the rice has rested off the heat for up to 5 minutes.

Garam masala

Pound the following ingredients to a powder with a pestle and mortar, or grind them in a clean coffee grinder (makes spare garam masala to store).

4 cloves	*1 tsp black peppercorns*
1 tsp cumin seeds	*seeds from 1 tsp cardamom*
2 cm (1 inch) of cinnamon	*pods*
1 tsp fennel seeds	*2 tsp coriander seeds*

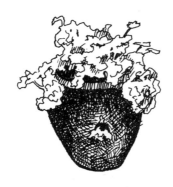

PASTA

Garganelli with morels

Garganelli are rolled pasta shapes made with egg and are sold either fresh or dried. Typical of the Emilia-Romagna region of northern Italy, they are especially popular in Bologna. Remembering the many delicious dishes of garganelli I have enjoyed on past visits to the annual Bologna children's book fair, I have created this spring recipe with seasonal morels, but any mushrooms can be substituted. This is an unashamedly rich combination that is quite delicious and worthy of Bologna's nickname of 'Bologna la grassa' – Bologna the fat. If you cannot find garganelli substitute penne or other short, hollow pasta shapes. Serves four with crusty bread and plenty of freshly grated parmesan.

225 g (8 oz) fresh morels or
40 g (1½ oz) dried morels
50 g (2 oz) unsalted butter
2 cloves of garlic, peeled and
finely chopped
3 shallots, peeled and
chopped
450 g (1 lb) dried garganelli
3 chopped, canned tomatoes
and their juice

salt
freshly milled black pepper
handful of fresh parsley,
washed and chopped
175 ml (6 fl oz) single cream
50 g (2 oz) parmesan,
freshly grated

If using dried morels soak them in a cup of hot water for 30 minutes. Strain and reserve the soaking liquid. If using fresh morels, halve them from top to bottom. Wash them well, to remove any grit.

Heat the butter in a pan and soften the garlic and shallots. Add the morels and sauté them for about 5 minutes. (If using dried morels, add the soaking liquid now and allow it to evaporate.)

Meanwhile, bring a very large pot of salted water to a boil. Drop in the garganelli and cook until they are *al dente*. (Take care not to overcook them.)

While the pasta cooks, add the tomatoes to the mushrooms and cook for 5 minutes, covered. Season and add the parsley and cream. Heat through and combine with the drained pasta. Serve.

Bucatini with oyster mushrooms

This is especially good with wild oyster or cornucopia mushrooms, with their pronounced woody taste, but is also very successful with the cultivated oyster mushrooms that are commonly available in supermarkets. Serves four.

350 g (12 oz) factory made bucatini or other long pasta strands
4 tbs extra virgin olive oil
275 g (10 oz) oyster mushrooms, trimmed and left whole, if small
3 cloves of garlic, peeled and thinly sliced
1 dried chilli, crumbled

6 tbs white wine
salt
freshly milled black pepper
generous handful of fresh parsley, washed and chopped
extra virgin olive oil
75 g (3 oz) freshly grated parmesan

Bring a very large pot of salted water to a rolling boil. Immerse the bucatini and stir well.

Heat the olive oil in a heavy pan; before it smokes add the mushrooms. Sear briefly, reduce the heat and sauté them for 3 minutes. Add the garlic, stir well and continue to sauté over a medium heat for 3 more minutes. Increase the heat again, add the wine and let it all but boil off. Season, and add the parsley and chilli. By now, the bucatini should be *al dente*. Drain the pasta, returning it to the empty pot, and pour the mushroom sauce over it, mixing well. Drizzle a little more extra virgin olive oil over the pasta. Serve with parmesan cheese, crusty bread and a green salad.

Fusilli with chestnut mushrooms

Any short, fat pasta shapes can be used instead of fusilli. Only use really fresh, firm mushrooms and serve as an excellent, quick appetizer for four, or a light meal for two people.

> 400 g (14 oz) packet fusilli
> 110 ml (4 fl oz) fruity olive oil
> 110 g (4 oz) pancetta or bacon, trimmed and diced
> 450 g (1 lb) chestnut mushrooms, cleaned and thickly sliced
>
> 2 cloves of garlic, peeled and chopped
> salt
> freshly milled black pepper
> generous handful of fresh parsley, washed and chopped
> freshly grated parmesan

Bring a very large pot of salted water to a vigorous boil; drop in the pasta and mix well. Cook until *al dente*.

While the pasta cooks, prepare the mushrooms. Heat half of the olive oil in a pan. Add the bacon and stir-fry for about 30 seconds. Before it turns crisp, add the mushrooms and mix well with the bacon. When, after a couple of minutes, the mushrooms have coloured lightly, add the garlic. Season and continue to sauté the mushrooms until they have reduced in bulk (this will take about 3 minutes). Remove from the heat until the pasta is tender.

Drain the pasta and transfer it to a warm serving dish. Quickly reheat the mushrooms and pour them over the pasta. Add the remaining oil and the parsley and mix everything thoroughly. Serve immediately with plenty of freshly grated parmesan cheese and crusty bread.

Linguine with ceps

Only the finest ingredients go into this simplest of dishes. It can also be made with lesser mushrooms but the results will be quite bland unless some dried ceps are first soaked in warm water and added with their strained soaking liquid, which should almost be allowed to boil away – in which case omit the stock. Serves four with freshly grated parmesan and good bread.

400 g (14 oz) factory made
linguine or spaghetti
110 g (4 oz) block of
unsalted butter
2 tbs olive oil
350 g (12 oz) fresh ceps,
sliced fairly thickly from
cap to stem base
2 cloves of garlic, peeled and
thinly sliced

2–4 tbs home-made chicken
stock (see p. 114)
salt
freshly milled black pepper
handful of fresh, flat-leaved
parsley, washed and
chopped
110 g (4 oz) freshly grated
parmesan

Bring a very large pot of salted water to a rolling boil and immerse the
pasta. Stir well and cook until *al dente*. Meanwhile, heat half of the
butter and all the olive oil in a heavy pan and add the ceps. Stir them
over a medium heat for 4 minutes, then reduce the heat, add the garlic
and stock and cook gently while the pasta cooks, stirring occasionally.
Season well, mix in the parsley and the remaining butter, and combine
thoroughly with the cooked, drained pasta, adding half of the parmesan. Serve with the remaining parmesan.

Tronchetti with ceps and walnuts

The first walnuts and ceps appear in the same season, and combine
deliciously. Alternatively, chestnut mushrooms and some dried ceps
can be used. Avoid stale, bitter walnuts, which will ruin the sauce.
Other pasta shapes can be substituted. Serves four with crusty bread
and a salad.

8 walnuts
225 g (8 oz) dried egg
tronchetti or 350 g
(12 oz) penne
175 g (6 oz) firm, young
ceps or 225 g (8 oz)
cultivated mushrooms and
18 g (¾ oz) reconstituted
dried ceps and their
strained soaking liquid
3 tbs extra virgin olive oil

2 cloves of garlic, peeled and
finely chopped
salt
freshly milled black pepper
3 tbs milk
3 tbs double cream
small handful of fresh
parsley, washed and
chopped
50 g (2 oz) parmesan,
freshly grated

Stand the walnuts upright on a solid surface, and tap the pointed ends
smartly with a hammer to smash the shells. Prise out the kernels and
chop them roughly.

Bring a very large pot of salted water to a rolling boil. Immerse the
pasta, mix well and boil until *al dente*.

Meanwhile, trim off the bottoms of the mushrooms and brush or wipe the caps clean. Slice them thinly. Heat the olive oil in a pan and gently fry the mushrooms for 4–5 minutes. Add the garlic and chopped walnuts, mix well and gently fry for 3 minutes longer. (Add the mushroom's soaking liquid now, if using, and boil it away.) Season, and pour in the milk and cream. Allow the sauce to thicken slightly, then mix in the parsley. (Turn off the heat now if the pasta is not yet ready.)

When the pasta is cooked, drain and combine thoroughly in the pan with the mushroom and walnut sauce, and mix in half of the parmesan. Serve immediately with the remaining parmesan in a separate bowl.

Penne with field mushrooms

This creamy mushroom sauce can be made with wild field mushrooms, or their delicious cousins, horse mushrooms. Alternatively, substitute cultivated open-cap mushrooms, combined with dried ceps that have been reconstituted by soaking in hot water for 20 minutes. (Reserve the strained soaking liquid, and add the ceps and their liquid to the pan after the thyme and garlic, allowing it to evaporate). Serves four.

400 g (14 oz) penne
25 g (1 oz) butter
2 tbs olive oil
350 g (12 oz) field or horse
mushrooms, sliced
4 sprigs of fresh thyme or a
pinch of dried thyme

2 cloves of garlic, chopped
6 tbs single cream
50 g (2 oz) freshly grated
parmesan

Bring abundant salted water to a rolling boil in a large pot. Add the penne and cook until *al dente*. Meanwhile, prepare the sauce. Heat the butter and olive oil in a pan. Fry the mushrooms over a high heat for 3–4 minutes, stirring continuously. Reduce the heat, add the thyme and garlic and fry gently for 2 more minutes. Add the cream and heat through. Remove the thyme stalks. Combine with the cooked, drained pasta and serve with freshly grated parmesan cheese.

Penne with mushrooms, ham and peas

Mushrooms, ham and peas combine very happily with stubby pasta shapes that are well lubricated with fruity olive oil. In season, use fresh peas and plum tomatoes; otherwise, substitute frozen peas and canned tomatoes. Make the full quantity for four people even if you are only serving two, as the leftovers can be used to make an excellent 'pasta al forno' (see below).

400 g (14 oz) factory-made
penne
4 shallots, peeled and
chopped
6 tbs extra virgin olive oil
350 g (12 oz) button
mushrooms, thickly sliced
2 cloves of garlic, peeled and
finely chopped
110 g (4 oz) lean cooked
ham, diced

175 g (6 oz) fresh, shelled or
frozen peas (thawed)
2 ripe plum tomatoes, peeled
and finely chopped or 2
canned plum tomatoes,
chopped
salt
freshly milled black pepper
50 g (2 oz) freshly grated
parmesan

Bring a very large pot of salted water to a rapid boil. Immerse the pasta, stirring well.

Meanwhile, gently fry the shallots in half of the oil. After a couple of minutes, and before the shallots colour, add the mushrooms. Sauté for 4 minutes. Add the garlic and ham, mix well, and raise the heat. Stir-fry for 2–3 minutes. Add the peas and tomatoes, reduce the heat and cook for 2–3 minutes longer. Season. By now, the pasta should be *al dente*. Drain the pasta well, combining it thoroughly with the mushrooms, ham and peas. Mix in the remaining olive oil and serve with freshly grated parmesan cheese.

Note: any leftover pasta can be combined in layers with a packet of Italian mozzarella (diced) and a generous sprinkling (50 g (2 oz)) of additional parmesan cheese. Bake at 190°C/375°F/gas mark 5 for about 20 minutes, or until golden.

Maccheroni with mushrooms and peas

This is best with the largest kinds of maccheroni, rigatoni or conchiglie. This simpler sauce without tomatoes relies on juicy mushrooms and the sweetness of peas, generously lubricated with extra virgin olive oil. Serves four as a starter, two as a light meal, with crusty bread and a salad.

6 tbs extra virgin olive oil
175 g (6 oz) button
* mushrooms, stems*
* trimmed and thickly sliced*
110 g (4 oz) fresh, or thawed
* frozen peas (shelled*
* weight)*
2 cloves garlic, peeled and
* sliced*

4 tbs white wine
225 g (8 oz) pasta
salt
freshly milled black pepper
handful of fresh parsley,
* washed and chopped*
50 g (2 oz) freshly grated
* parmesan*

Heat half of the oil in a non-stick pan. Add the mushrooms. Fry them for 2 minutes, then add the peas. Mix well, reduce the heat and continue to sauté for 2 minutes longer. Add the garlic, stir for 1 minute and add the wine. Reduce (this will only take a minute). Meanwhile, cook the pasta in a large pot of salted water. When *al dente*, drain and return the pasta to the empty pot. Reheat the sauce, season well and sprinkle with parsley. Combine with the pasta and the remaining olive oil. Serve with freshly grated parmesan cheese.

Linguine alla puttanesca

Neapolitan prostitutes are said to have invented a sauce containing tomatoes, garlic, black olives, capers and anchovies; this would certainly account for its name. I prefer the muskiness of mushrooms to the salty flavour of anchovies, adding a bite of chilli and some fresh basil, which combined contribute a special quality to a steaming dish of linguine or spaghetti. Serves four.

400 g (14 oz) factory-made
linguine or spaghetti
6 tbs extra virgin olive oil
2 cloves of garlic, peeled and
chopped
1 dried chilli, crumbled
225 g (8 oz) mushrooms,
wiped clean and sliced
salt

110 ml (4 fl oz) tomato
passata
a little water
2 tsp capers, rinsed and
drained
12 stoned black olives,
quartered
handful of fresh basil, washed
and chopped

Bring a very large pot of salted water to a rapid boil. Immerse the pasta and cook until *al dente*.

Meanwhile, heat the olive oil in a pan, add the garlic, chilli and mushrooms and stir-fry them over a medium heat for 5 minutes. Season and add the tomato passata, a little water, the capers and olives. Cover and simmer the sauce while the pasta cooks, removing it from the heat after 5 minutes or so. When the pasta is tender, drain it well and reheat the sauce briefly. Combine the sauce thoroughly with the pasta, sprinkle with the basil and serve with crusty bread.

Baked pasta with shiitake

Cultivated shiitake mushrooms are delicious in this warming baked pasta dish which serves four.

400 g (14 oz) rigatoni or
short, chunky maccheroni
olive oil for frying
1 medium aubergine,
trimmed and sliced into
thin wedges
4 tbs extra virgin olive oil
110 g (4 oz) shiitake
mushrooms, stems
trimmed, halved
400 g (14 oz) can of plum
tomatoes, crushed

2 cloves of garlic, peeled and
chopped
salt
freshly milled black pepper
generous handful of basil,
washed
1 packet of mozzarella, diced
110 g (4 oz) parmesan,
grated

Preheat the oven to 220°C/425°F/gas mark 7. Bring plenty of salted water to the boil. Drop in the pasta and boil until nearly tender but not quite *al dente*. While this is cooking, heat plenty of olive oil to smoking point in a non-stick or well seasoned frying pan. Add the aubergines and fry them until golden, turning once or twice. Remove with a slotted spoon and drain them on kitchen paper.

Heat the extra virgin olive oil in another pan and add the mushrooms. Sauté them for 4 minutes, then add the tomatoes and garlic. Continue to simmer until the sauce has reduced (about 10 more minutes). Season with salt and freshly milled black pepper, remove from the heat and add the basil. Oil a deep-sided ovenproof gratin dish and put in a layer of the mushroom, tomato and basil sauce. Cover with a layer of partly cooked, drained pasta, scatter with fried aubergines, then top with morsels of mozzarella and a sprinkling of parmesan. Repeat until the ingredients are used up. Bake for 15–20 minutes, or until the final topping of cheese is golden. Serve with crusty bread and a salad.

Rigatoni al funghetto

'Al funghetto' is a term used to describe aubergines that are cooked in such a way as to make them taste mushroomy. You may, of course, add some mushrooms for good measure! Serves four.

6 tbs olive oil
1 aubergine, washed, trimmed and diced into 1 cm (½ inch) cubes
1 small onion, peeled and diced
225 g (8 oz) button mushrooms, quartered (optional)
2 cloves of garlic, peeled and finely chopped
1 anchovy fillet, rinsed and finely chopped

3 sprigs of fresh thyme or a pinch of dried thyme
6 tbs dry white wine
400 g (14 oz) can of tomatoes, chopped
salt
freshly milled black pepper
575 g (1¼ lb) rigatoni or other large, hollow pasta shapes
50 g (2 oz) freshly grated parmesan

Heat half of the oil in a non-stick pan and when it starts to smoke, add the aubergine. Toss until it begins to brown, then reserve it. Heat the remaining oil in the same pan and sauté the onion until translucent. Add the mushrooms (if using) and the garlic and anchovy. Continue to sauté for a few more minutes, then return the aubergines to the pan and add the thyme and white wine. Allow the wine partly to evaporate and add the tomatoes. Simmer very gently for 15 minutes and season.

While the sauce is cooking, heat plenty of salted water in a large pot. When at a rolling boil, add the pasta. Cook until *al dente*. Drain the pasta well and combine it thoroughly with the sauce. Serve with freshly grated parmesan.

Spaghettini with summer truffles

Summer truffles grow in the southern counties of England, especially in chalky districts under oak and beech, and have some of the rude pungency of white and black truffles at a fraction of the cost. Nonetheless, they are expensive and rare. I combine them with other fungi to eke them out, and, in any case, it is more their aroma than their substance that counts. Like their more expensive cousins, summer truffles are superb with pasta, but you can substitute truffle-flavoured oil. These quantities serve two.

2–4 summer truffles (about 17 g (²⁄₃ oz) in total), or a little truffle oil
250 g (9 oz) spaghettini or spaghetti
75 g (3 oz) unsalted butter
75 g (3 oz) oyster or shiitake mushrooms, cleaned, trimmed and sliced
12 g (½ oz) reconstituted dried ceps or morels and their strained soaking liquid (allow 20 minutes to soak ceps, 30 for morels)

1 clove of garlic, peeled and chopped
handful of fresh parsley, washed and chopped
salt
freshly milled black pepper
50 g (2 oz) freshly grated parmesan

Shave off the hard, knobbly outer 'skin' of the truffles with a very sharp knife, taking care to retain as much of the flesh as possible.

Heat a large pot of salted water. When it reaches a rolling boil, immerse the spaghettini and mix well. Cook until *al dente*.

Meanwhile, prepare the sauce. Melt half of the butter in a large pan. Add the fresh mushrooms and gently fry them over a medium heat for 2–3 minutes. Add the dried mushrooms and their soaking liquid, the garlic and parsley. Season and simmer until the pasta is tender. Drain the pasta and combine with the remaining butter, mixing thoroughly with the mushrooms. Grate the truffles over the pasta with the coarsest blade on a grater, or slice them as thin as possible and scatter them over the dish. Alternatively, add 1-2 tbs of truffle oil and mix well. Serve immediately with parmesan cheese.

Linguine with truffle oil

This is my favourite pasta creation and an excellent, economical way to savour the unique aroma and flavour of white Alba truffles. Although truffle oil is extremely expensive (a tiny bottle will set you back about £8), only a tablespoon is required to transform a plate of mushrooms and pasta and, unlike fresh truffles, the highly flavoured oil will keep for a few months. Spaghetti, spaghettini, bucatini and trenette can all be substituted. Serves two.

225 g (8 oz) factory-made
   linguine
25 g (1 oz) butter
1 tbs extra virgin olive oil
175 g (6 oz) shiitake and
   chestnut mushrooms,
   sliced
12 g (½ oz) reconstituted
   dried ceps or morels and
   their strained soaking
   liquid (allow 20 minutes
   to soak ceps, 30 for morels)

2 cloves of garlic, peeled and
   chopped
handful of fresh parsley,
   washed and chopped
salt
freshly milled black pepper
splash of white wine
50 g (2 oz) parmesan,
   freshly grated
1 tbs truffle oil

Bring a large pot of salted water to a vigorous boil and immerse the linguine. Cook until *al dente*.

    Meanwhile, prepare the sauce by heating the butter and olive oil in a small frying pan. Add the mushrooms and sear over a high heat to gild the edges, then cook more gently for 3–4 minutes longer. Mix in the garlic and parsley, season and sauté for another minute. Add the soaking liquid and a generous splash of white wine and allow most of the liquid to evaporate. Reserve. When the pasta is tender, drain it and return it to the empty pot. Mix in the mushroom sauce (briefly reheated, if necessary) and mix in all the parmesan and the truffle oil. Combine very thoroughly and serve with crusty bread and a green salad.

Fresh egg pasta

Although this recipe contains no mushrooms, you may like to make your own fresh pasta and serve it with any of the mushroom sauces in this book.

300 g (11 oz) extra-fine	*1 tsp salt*
plain flour	*1 tbs olive oil*
3 eggs	

Pour the flour into a bowl and make a well in the centre. Break the eggs into the well, add the salt and olive oil. Knead with floured hands (for 15 minutes), or with a machine fitted with dough hooks (for 4–5 minutes), or in a food processor (the dough will rapidly roll up into a smooth ball and will require a couple of minutes' hand-kneading). Apply a little more flour to the dough which should be elastic and smooth.

Apply a sprinkling of flour to a large, clean work surface and sprinkle your rolling pin with flour. Roll out the dough as thinly as possible without breaking it. Sprinkle with flour. Let the dough dry out for about 25 minutes, then roll it up, as you would a carpet, and cut it crossways at narrow, equal intervals, according to the desired width, either with a sharp knife, or with a pastry wheel if you want the noodles to have saw-toothed edges. Unravel the noodles, dust them with a little flour and carefully drape them over the back of a chair. If you wish to use them fresh, they will be ready after 10 minutes' drying. If you want to store the pasta, let it dry out completely overnight. (Once dried, it will keep almost indefinitely.)

Cook the pasta until tender in a very large pot of rapidly boiling salted water to which you have added a few drops of oil. Drain and serve with a sauce.

Mushroom sauce for fresh egg pasta

50 g (2 oz) butter
2 tbs porcini oil (see recipe
    on p. 111) or extra virgin
    olive oil
2 cloves of garlic, peeled and
    chopped
175 g (6 oz) fresh
    mushrooms, thinly sliced

salt
freshly milled black pepper
280 ml (10 fl oz) double
    cream
2 handfuls of fresh parsley,
    washed and chopped
110 g (4 oz) parmesan,
    freshly grated

Melt the butter in a pan with the porcini or olive oil and the garlic. Add the mushrooms. Cook over a high heat for a minute, then reduce the heat and continue to cook for about 3 minutes (remove from the heat until the pasta is almost ready). Before the pasta is tender, season the mushrooms, return the pan to the heat, and add the cream. Cook for a minute or so, to thicken the cream. Add the parsley and mix well. Drain and return the pasta to the pot (or transfer to a warm serving bowl). Mix in the sauce and half of the parmesan, and serve with the remaining cheese.

Wild-mushroom-flavoured fresh pasta

25 g (1 oz) reconstituted
    dried ceps and their
    strained soaking liquid
400–450 g (14–16 oz)
    extra-fine plain flour

3 eggs
1 tsp salt

Process the ceps with their soaking liquid in a food processor. Pour all but 75 g (3 oz) of the flour into a bowl and make a well in the centre. Break the eggs into the well, and add the salt and the mushroom paste. Proceed to make the pasta as directed on p. 65. When *al dente*, serve with the sauce below, or dress with a little porcini or truffle oil and some freshly grated parmesan.

Sauce for wild mushroom-flavoured pasta

Simmer some sprigs of fresh sage, thyme and rosemary in butter with 2 peeled and crushed gloves of garlic. Discard the garlic before it burns and season with freshly milled black pepper. Add freshly grated parmesan cheese.

Ravioli of wild mushrooms

This makes four large ravioli, one for each person; each raviolo is stuffed with a mixture of wild and cultivated mushrooms and served in a simple sauce of seasoned melted butter and parmesan cheese. Serve with crusty bread and a salad of dressed frisée and radicchio leaves.

Make the pasta dough as directed on p. 65. Knead and roll out, but do not roll it up and cut it. While the dough rests, make the filling.

Filling

40 g (1½ oz) butter
1 tbs olive oil
3 shallots, peeled and
   coarsely chopped
12 g (½ oz) reconstituted
   dried ceps and their
   strained soaking liquid

175 g (6 oz) mushrooms,
   thinly sliced
sprig of thyme
3 tbs white wine
salt
freshly milled black pepper

Heat the butter and olive oil in a pan. Add the shallots and fry them until soft. Raise the heat, add the wild and cultivated mushrooms and the thyme, and sear for about 3 minutes; reduce the heat and gently sauté the mushrooms for a few minutes longer. Add the soaking liquid and the wine, raise the heat and allow the liquid to evaporate. Season, and remove the thyme. Allow the mixture to cool.

Cut out eight dough rectangles, each measuring approximately 7½ cm (3 inches) x 10 cm (4 inches) (the surplus trimmings can be reserved and cut into noodles). Spoon the filling on to the centres of four of the sheets. Moisten the edges of the filled sheets with a little water. Cover with the four remaining sheets and pinch the edges together to seal them (ensure they are completely sealed).

Bring a large pot of salted water to the boil, adding a few drops of oil. Boil the ravioli for 10 minutes.

Sauce

75 g (3 oz) butter
1 clove of garlic, peeled and
   lightly crushed
freshly milled black pepper
75 g (3 oz) parmesan,
   freshly grated

handful of fresh parsley,
   washed and chopped
a few drops of truffle oil
   (optional)

A minute or two before the ravioli are tender, melt the butter in a pan with the crushed garlic clove, season with plenty of freshly milled black pepper and a simmer for a minute or two. When cooked, drain the ravioli carefully and transfer to four warm plates. Discard the garlic and pour the seasoned butter over each raviolo, adding a generous sprinkling of freshly grated parmesan and parsley (and if desired, a few drops of truffle oil). Serve immediately.

SALADS

Salad of chestnut mushrooms and beans

Chestnut mushrooms taste more 'mushroomy' than ordinary buttons and their firm texture while still very fresh makes them an excellent choice for eating raw. Here, the various textures are contrastingly soft and crunchy.

400 g (14 oz) canned cannellini beans, rinsed and drained
250 g (9 oz) chestnut mushrooms, wiped clean and thinly sliced
2–3 tender hearts of celery, washed and thinly sliced
1 firm tomato, washed and diced

4–6 leaves of wild garlic or green spring onion leaves or a handful of chives, washed and sliced
1 clove of garlic, crushed
6 tbs extra virgin olive oil
1 tbs balsamic vinegar
1 tsp salt

Combine the beans with the mushrooms, celery, tomato and leaves in a bowl. Beat the garlic with the oil, vinegar and salt and pour over the salad. Mix thoroughly and serve with crusty bread.

Salad of ceps

This fine salad calls for the firmest young ceps in peak condition and is fit for a king and queen. (Alternatively, substitute very fresh cultivated chestnut mushrooms.) I relish this especially when I have picked the first ceps of late summer; indeed, I write after a successful expedition, duly rewarded with a few prize specimens that are just right for this recipe. Serves two.

3 very firm ceps (about 250 g (9 oz) in total), wiped clean
juice of half a lemon
a few bitter leaves (rocket, radicchio, dandelion, chicory)
a few leaves of watercress
heart of a Cos lettuce, washed, drained and patted dry

olive oil for frying
1 clove of garlic, peeled and lightly crushed
1 slice of stale bread, cubed
1 tbs balsamic vinegar
4 tbs extra virgin olive oil or porcini oil (see recipe on p. 111)
salt
1 tsp fresh chives, washed and snipped

Trim off the very bottoms of the stems of the ceps. Slice very thinly from the caps to the bottom of the stems and place them in a bowl. Sprinkle with the lemon juice, mix well and set aside for 10–15 minutes.

Arrange the leaves, watercress and lettuce heart in a salad bowl. Heat the olive oil in a small, non-stick frying pan and when it starts to smoke, drop in the garlic. Swirl it around and remove when it has coloured a little. Add the bread. Fry until golden, remove, drain, and reserve on kitchen paper. Gently combine the sliced ceps with the salad leaves and scatter the croûtons over them. Beat the balsamic vinegar with the extra virgin olive oil or porcini oil and salt, and pour over the salad, mixing gently but thoroughly, without breaking the ceps. Sprinkle with the chives and serve.

Fresh sweetcorn salad with bay boletus

An early autumn salad created to celebrate an abundance of plump sweetcorn and firm little bay boletus mushrooms (or very firm small ceps). This recipe serves two accompanied by bread. Crisp button mushrooms may be substituted.

4 whole cobs of sweetcorn
4 tbs extra virgin olive oil
2 tbs red wine or sherry
 vinegar
6–8 bay boleti, wiped clean
 and thinly sliced

salt
generous handful of fresh
 coriander, washed and
 chopped

Remove the papery skins and stringy fibres from the corn cobs. With a very sharp knife, make vertical cuts along each row of corn kernels (this will facilitate their removal). Slice the kernels off the cobs, transfer them to a small pan of salted water and boil until tender (12–15 minutes). Drain them well and transfer to a serving bowl. Beat the olive oil with the vinegar. Mix in the remaining ingredients, pour the dressing over them and serve when cooled.

Salad of button mushrooms with rocket and peppers

This colourful salad has a pleasantly tart flavour and serves two.

225 g (8 oz) crisp button
 mushrooms
juice of ½ lemon
1 green pepper, seeded and
 diced
1 red or yellow pepper,
 seeded and diced

6–8 rocket leaves
4 tbs extra virgin olive oil
1 tbs white wine vinegar
salt
freshly milled black pepper
1 tsp mustard

Trim the stalks off the button mushrooms and slice them finely. Place them in a bowl with the lemon juice, mixing well. Add the peppers and rocket leaves. Beat the oil with the vinegar, seasoning and mustard. Pour over the salad and mix well. Serve immediately.

Oyster mushroom salad

Whenever I am lucky enough to find them I collect aromatic white cornucopia and oyster mushrooms that grow wild on dead wood, otherwise substituting the yellow, pink and grey oyster mushrooms that are sold in large supermarkets.

1 sweet red pepper, washed
225 g (8 oz) mixed oyster
mushrooms
2 'Little Gem' lettuces (or
heart of a Cos lettuce),
washed and sliced
4 spring onions, washed and
sliced
6 rocket leaves, washed and
torn

6 sun-dried tomato halves
preserved in oil, drained
and sliced thinly
4 tbs extra virgin olive oil
1 tbs wine vinegar
salt
½ tsp sugar
1 tsp mustard

Remove and discard the pepper's cap, white pithy membrane and seeds. Dice the flesh. Trim off the mushrooms' tough stem bottoms. Slice large caps but leave small ones whole. Pat all the washed vegetables dry with kitchen paper and combine them thoroughly in a salad bowl with the mushrooms and sun-dried tomatoes. Beat the oil with the vinegar, salt, sugar and mustard. Pour over the salad and mix all the ingredients thoroughly, to ensure that everything is well coated with the dressing. Serve this colourful and very tasty salad immediately.

Rice salad with mushrooms

A fairly substantial salad that calls for cold, cooked rice. A golden version can be made with cold saffron pilaff (long-grain rice that has been boiled in aromatic chicken or vegetable stock, infused with saffron). Serves two as a light meal, four as an accompaniment or appetizer.

675 g (1½ lb) cooked long-
grain rice
3 spring onions, sliced
1 'Little Gem' lettuce,
washed, drained and
shredded
handful of fresh parsley,
washed and chopped
2 tbs olive oil

175 g (6 oz) button
mushrooms, thinly sliced
stick of celery, washed and
sliced
1 red pepper, seeds and pith
removed, diced
3 tbs extra virgin olive oil
1½ tbs wine vinegar
1 tsp salt

Combine the rice, spring onions, lettuce and parsley. Heat the olive oil in a frying pan. Stir-fry the mushrooms, celery and pepper over a high heat for about 3 minutes, until just wilted. Remove with a slotted spoon and combine them with the rice. Beat the oil, vinegar and salt and pour over the salad. Mix thoroughly but gently, cover, and set aside for at least an hour (preferably longer) to allow the flavours to develop.

Variation

Separately boil 2–3 tbs of wild rice until tender; this will take about 40 minutes. Fold the grains into the rice salad.

SOUPS

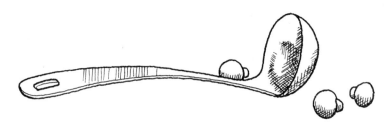

Cream of mushroom soup

This soup is made with a combination of cultivated and dried wild mushrooms and is therefore good for year-round use. I prefer to use large, open-cap mushrooms with pinkish-brown gills (older specimens with chocolate-coloured gills give the soup an unappetizing dark colour). This will freeze well, without the cream; add it to the soup when you reheat it.

50 g (2 oz) butter
3–4 shallots, peeled and chopped
25 g (1 oz) reconstituted dried ceps or morels and their strained soaking liquid (allow 20 minutes to soak ceps, 30 for morels)
350 g (12 oz) mushrooms, roughly chopped

1 litre (1¾ pints) home-made chicken stock (see recipe on p. 114)
small wine glass of dry sherry
salt
freshly milled black pepper
110 ml (4 fl oz) single cream

Melt the butter with the shallots. Stir them around until they have softened. Add the reconstituted and fresh mushrooms and stir-fry them for 5 minutes. Add the stock, sherry, and the mushrooms' soaking liquid. Season, and mix well. Bring to a boil, then reduce the heat, cover and simmer for half an hour. Allow the soup to cool, then blend in a food processor until smooth. Reheat gently without boiling, stir in the cream, and serve with crusty bread or croûtons.

Variation

Slice the mushrooms thinly. Proceed as above, but instead of blending the soup, strain the liquid, retaining the mushrooms. Return them to the soup and reheat.

Wild mushroom soup

Here is a standard recipe for a quite delicious soup that can be made with wild field or horse mushrooms, or cultivated open cap mushrooms (either way, very fresh ones with pale gills are preferable to older ones with dark gills. This serves four people.

25 g (2 oz) butter
2 tbs olive oil
1 medium onion, peeled and
    chopped
1 clove of garlic, peeled and
    chopped
350 g (12 oz) field or horse
    mushrooms or
    350 g (12 oz) open cap
    cultivated mushrooms and
    12 g (½ oz) reconstituted
    dried ceps and their
    strained soaking liquid

1 ripe tomato, peeled and
    diced
salt
freshly milled black pepper
900 ml (1½ pints) home-
    made chicken stock (see
    recipe on p. 114)
handful of fresh parsley,
    washed and chopped

Melt the butter in a large pot with the olive oil. Add the onion and fry until lightly coloured and soft. Add the garlic, mix well, and add the fresh mushrooms. Sauté over a medium heat until they have reduced in bulk by half (4–5 minutes). Add the tomato and cook for a minute. (If using, add the dried mushrooms and their strained soaking liquid now.) Season well. Add the stock and bring to a simmer. Cook, covered, for 25 minutes. Allow to cool. Blend the soup to a smooth consistency in a food processor. Reheat it gently, stirring in the parsley just before serving with crusty bread or croûtons.

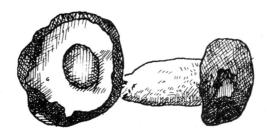

Cep soup

This excellent soup is best with fresh ceps; otherwise, use reconstituted dried ceps and their strained soaking liquid and replace the ceps with cultivated open-cap mushrooms, proceeding as directed. Serves four to six.

3 tbs olive oil
25 g (1 oz) butter
1 onion, peeled and chopped
450 g (1 lb) fresh ceps,
    cleaned and chopped or
    450 g (1 lb) open cap
    mushrooms, chopped and
    16 g (⅔ oz) reconstituted
    dried ceps and their
    strained soaking liquid

2 cloves of garlic, peeled and
    chopped
salt
freshly milled black pepper
1350 ml (2½ pints) home-
    made chicken stock (see
    recipe on p. 114)

Heat the oil and butter in a capacious pot and soften the onion, stirring well. Add the mushrooms and fry for 5 minutes, stirring all the time. Add the garlic and cook for a minute longer. Season. Pour in the stock (and the ceps' soaking liquid, if using). Bring to the boil, cover, reduce the heat and simmer for 20 minutes. Uncover and let the soup cool. Process until smooth, return to the pot and reheat the soup gently. Correct the seasoning and serve with crusty bread or croûtons.

Mushroom soup with pearl barley

Mushrooms and pearl barley combine very pleasantly in this comforting Polish soup in which dried ceps are indispensable. The pearl barley gives a wonderful soft texture. Serves six.

3 tbs sunflower oil
1 onion, peeled and chopped
small carrot, scrubbed and
    diced
16 g (⅔ oz) reconstituted
    dried ceps, chopped, and
    their strained soaking
    liquid
4 tbs mushroom duxelles (see
    recipe on p. 112)

1½ litres (2¾ pints) home-
    made chicken stock (see
    recipe on p. 114)
110 g (4 oz) pearl barley
salt
freshly milled black pepper
handful of fresh parsley,
    washed and chopped
6 tbs soured cream (optional)

Heat the oil in a pot. Fry the onion and carrot until lightly coloured and soft. Stir in the ceps and the duxelles. (If you do not have the duxelles, fry 225 g (8 oz) of finely chopped mushrooms in butter with a peeled and chopped shallot until all the moisture has been shed and evaporated; season and sprinkle with parsley. Add the mixture to the pot.)

Pour in the stock and the ceps' soaking liquid. Add the pearl barley. Season, bring to a simmer, cover and cook for about 1½ hours. Stir in the parsley, check the seasoning and, if desired, stir in the soured cream. Serve with buttered rye bread.

Barsch with mushroom dumplings

This very refined Polish beetroot consommé is always served on Christmas Eve (the feast of *Wigilia*), with such meatless delicacies as marinated herrings with soured cream, carp, and various salads. It is a beautiful ruby colour and, unlike Ukrainian *borscht*, this is a strained soup, to which the vegetables contribute just their colour and flavour. It serves six with little mushroom-filled dumplings. Resist the temptation to use pre-cooked beetroot: only fresh ones will do.

> 575 g (1¼ lb) fresh beetroot,
>   sliced
> 1 small celeriac, peeled and
>   sliced
> 1½ litres (2¾ pints) home-
>   made vegetable stock (see
>   recipe on p. 114)
> 1 onion, peeled and halved
>
> 2 cloves of garlic, peeled
> 4–6 parsley stalks, with
>   leaves attached
> 25 g (1 oz) dried ceps
> juice of half a lemon
> 2 tsp sugar
> salt

Combine everything except the lemon juice, sugar and salt in a pot, cover, and simmer for an hour. Strain into another pot and add the flavourings. Extract and reserve the mushrooms. Reheat the soup gently and serve hot with mushroom dumplings.

Mushroom dumplings

> 200 g (7 oz) plain flour
> 2 eggs
> ½ tsp salt
> 2 tbs olive oil
> 1 small onion, peeled and
>   chopped
> the wild mushrooms used to
>   flavour the barsch
>
> 175 g (6 oz) wild or
>   cultivated mushrooms,
>   diced
> generous handful each of
>   fresh parsley and dill,
>   washed and chopped
> salt
> freshly milled black pepper

In a food processor, blend the flour, eggs and salt briefly. The dough should roll up into a ball. Knead by hand for about 5 more minutes, then let it rest for 15 minutes. Roll it out thinly on a floured work surface. Cut the sheet into 4 cm (2 inch) squares.

Heat the oil in a small pan, add the onions and soften. Add the mushrooms. Sauté over a high heat for 6–8 minutes, then add the parsley and dill. Season and remove from the heat. When the mixture has cooled a little, spoon a small mound into the centres of half of the squares of dough. Place the remaining squares over them and pinch the edges together, moistening them with a little water. (Ensure that all edges are completely sealed in this way: they must be absolutely welded together, or they will disgorge their contents when boiled.)

Bring a large pot of water to the boil, reduce the heat, and simmer the dumplings for 6–8 minutes or until tender. Drain and serve them in the soup bowls, ladling the *barsch* over them.

Vegetarian hot and sour soup

While purists would insist on using chicken's or duck's blood and pork, my version of this very popular peasant soup from northern China substitutes plenty of bean curd, dried and fresh mushrooms, and a dash of bitingly hot chilli oil. Dried shiitake mushrooms are very concentrated in flavour and can be found in oriental shops. The soup is garnished with aromatic coriander. Serves four.

40 g (1½ oz) dried shiitake mushrooms	2 tsp sugar
25 g (1 oz) thin rice noodles	salt
1 litre (1¾ pints) home-made vegetable stock (see recipe on p. 114)	freshly milled black pepper
	4 spring onions, thinly sliced
	1 tbs flour mixed with 2 tbs water
75 g (3 oz) fresh young oyster mushrooms, diced	2 eggs, beaten
250 g (9 oz) fresh bean curd cakes, finely diced	1 tbs sesame oil
	1–2 tsp chilli oil (to taste)
2 tbs light soy sauce	handful of fresh coriander, washed and chopped
1 tbs dark soy sauce	
4 tbs rice vinegar	2–3 green chillies, seeded and thinly sliced (optional)
2 tbs Shaohsing wine or sherry	

Soak the shiitake mushrooms in hot water for 30 minutes to reconstitute them. Strain and reserve the water. Slice the shiitake caps very thinly, discarding the tough stalks. Meanwhile, bring a pot of water to the boil. Immerse the noodles and boil for the recommended period (usually 3–5 minutes). Drain and reserve them.

Bring the stock and the mushrooms' soaking liquid to a boil in a large pot. Add the reconstituted and fresh mushrooms, the noodles, bean curd, soy sauces, vinegar, Shaohsing wine, sugar, seasoning and the spring onions. Return to the boil, reduce the heat, and simmer for 3–4 minutes, then add the flour dissolved in water, stir, and allow the soup to thicken a little. Stir in the beaten eggs in a very thin stream and pull in different directions with a fork, to stretch the eggs as they set. Add the sesame and chilli oils, mix, and simmer for a minute longer. Serve garnished with coriander and the chillies (if using).

VEGETABLE ACCOMPANIMENTS

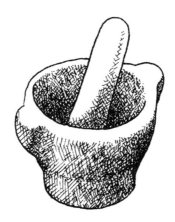

French mushroom sauce

Serve this classic French mushroom sauce with any meat dish, or try it with pasta. (Admittedly, the soy sauce is a less than classical element but I find that it imparts depth to the flavour of the sauce.) These quantities serve four.

40 g (1½ oz) butter
2–3 shallots, peeled and
  finely chopped
350 g (12 oz) button
  mushrooms, cleaned and
  thinly sliced
clove of garlic, peeled and
  finely chopped
6 tbs white wine

280 ml (10 fl oz) home-made
  chicken stock (see recipe on
  p. 114)
1 tbs tomato purée
1 tbs light soy sauce
pinch of salt
freshly milled black pepper
fresh parsley and chives,
  washed and chopped

Melt half of the butter in a pan. Sweat the shallots until soft and lightly coloured, then add the mushrooms and garlic. Stir-fry over a medium heat until the mushrooms have reduced (about 6 minutes). Pour in the wine, stock, tomato purée and soy sauce. Season lightly – the soy sauce is salty – and mix well. Increase the heat and boil down to a thick sauce (this will take about 20 minutes). Stir in the remaining butter and the herbs and mix thoroughly. Serve hot.

Garlicky button mushrooms

Choose very fresh, firm buttons for this simple recipe, which serves four as a vegetable accompaniment.

400 g (14 oz) button
mushrooms, wiped clean
and halved
3 tbs olive oil
3 cloves of garlic, peeled and
thinly sliced

2 tbs lemon juice
salt
freshly milled black pepper
handful of fresh parsley,
washed and chopped

Sauté the mushrooms in the oil until lightly coloured. Add the garlic and lemon juice; season. Mix well and cook gently for 2–3 minutes. Mix in the parsley and serve immediately.

Sautéed button mushrooms with pine nuts

Serve these tasty mushrooms as a vegetable accompaniment for four, or as an antipasto.

4 tbs olive oil
small onion, peeled and
chopped
3 slices lean bacon, trimmed
and diced
350 g (12 oz) firm button
mushrooms, wiped clean
2 cloves of garlic, peeled and
finely chopped

2 tbs pine nuts
140 ml (5 fl oz) white wine
1 tbs brandy
salt
freshly milled black pepper
handful of parsley, washed
and chopped

Heat the oil. Fry the onion and bacon for a minute until lightly coloured. Add the button mushrooms and stir-fry over a high heat for 30 seconds; add the garlic and pine nuts, lower the heat and cook gently for about 3 minutes. Pour in the wine and brandy, season and allow the liquid to reduce by over two-thirds. Serve sprinkled with parsley.

Funghi trifolati

The origins of the name of this dish are uncertain; *trifolare* may mean 'to cook in the manner of truffles'. Stronger-flavoured flat-leaved parsley is best. Use a mixture or a single variety of wild mushrooms or substitute cultivated oyster, chestnut and shiitake mushrooms. Serves two as an appetizer, four as a vegetable accompaniment.

3 tbs extra virgin olive oil
1 dried red chilli, crumbled
350 g (12 oz) mushrooms,
cleaned and sliced (not too
thinly)
2 cloves of garlic, peeled and
chopped

salt
freshly milled black pepper
the leaves from 4–6 sprigs of
parsley, washed and
chopped

Heat the oil in a well-seasoned or non-stick frying pan. Add the chilli and the mushrooms and sauté over a medium heat for 5–6 minutes, turning them in the oil frequently. Add the garlic, season and continue to sauté for 2 more minutes. Throw in the parsley, mix well, and serve.

Sautéed shiitake mushrooms

Shiitake mushrooms have been cultivated in the orient for over a thousand years, and are chiefly used in their dried form (the best are from Japan). Recently they have become available fresh and taste more like wild mushrooms than the other cultivated species. They are perhaps best quickly sautéed, as here. Fresh ceps are also delicious sautéed like this. Serves two.

350 g (12 oz) shiitake
mushrooms, stems
trimmed
4 tbs virgin olive oil
2 cloves of garlic, peeled and
chopped

½ dried chilli, crumbled
(optional)
salt
freshly milled black pepper
generous handful of fresh
parsley

Slice the shiitake mushrooms thickly. Heat the oil in a well-seasoned or non-stick frying pan to smoking point. Add the mushrooms. Sear them briefly, then reduce the heat and sauté for 3–4 minutes. Add the garlic, the chilli (if using), seasoning and parsley. Mix well. Serve while still very hot.

Mushrooms in sherry sauce

Serve this rich, creamy sauce as a vegetable accompaniment to roasts and grills, use it as a filling for pastry or brioches, or serve on buttered toast. Serves four.

12 g (½ oz) dried ceps
50 g (2 oz) butter
400 g (14 oz) button
*   mushrooms, quartered*
4 shallots, peeled and
*   chopped*
salt
freshly milled black pepper

pinch of dried thyme
1 tbs tomato purée, dissolved
*   in 350 ml (12 fl oz) home-*
*   made vegetable stock (see*
*   recipe on p. 114)*
4 tbs dry sherry
4 tbs double cream

Soak the ceps in a cup of hot water for 20 minutes. Strain and reserve their soaking liquid. Melt the butter in a pan. Sauté all the mushrooms and shallots until lightly coloured. Season. Add the thyme and continue to fry gently for a few minutes. Add the ceps' soaking liquid, pour in the tomato-rich stock and the sherry and bring to the boil. Reduce to a simmer and cook slowly until the sauce has reduced by half (12–15 minutes). Stir in the cream, heat for a minute to thicken, and serve.

Ragoût of oyster mushrooms and vegetables

Serve this substantial vegetable stew with crusty bread, or as an accompaniment to roasted or grilled meat, poultry or fish. Serves four.

6 tbs olive oil
2 medium, all-purpose
*   potatoes, peeled and diced*
1 medium onion, peeled and
*   chopped*
2 courgettes, washed and
*   sliced into thin segments*
350 g (12 oz) oyster
*   mushrooms, cleaned, stems*
*   trimmed, and sliced*

2 cloves of garlic, peeled and
*   finely chopped*
salt
1 tbs paprika
pinch of cayenne pepper
*   (optional)*
6 tbs white wine
4 tbs tomato passata
handful of fresh parsley,
*   washed and chopped*

Heat the olive oil to smoking point in a heavy pan. Add the potatoes and fry them until evenly golden, turning them in the oil several times. Add the onion and courgettes, reduce the heat, and fry gently until the vegetables are lightly coloured. Add the mushrooms and garlic, mix well and fry gently for about 5 more minutes, by which time the mushrooms will have reduced in bulk by half. Season. Add the paprika and cayenne pepper (if using), mix, and add the wine and tomato. Cover the pan and cook gently for 5 more minutes. (Moisten with a little water if the pan dries out.) Sprinkle with parsley and serve.

Stir-fried chicken of the woods with broccoli

Chicken of the woods is a startling yellow tree-fungus with an orange underbelly that, when sliced, really does look and taste like chicken breast. It favours oak, cherry, sweet chestnut, ash and willow but often grows high up on the trunk, or on branches. Only very young, juicy specimens should be eaten – older ones are tough and sour. This recipe serves two as an accompaniment to an oriental dish with rice.

2 tbs peanut oil	½ tsp sugar
110 g (4 oz) chicken of the	salt
woods, thinly sliced	2 tbs Shaohsing wine
175 g (6 oz) broccoli florets	4 tbs water
and their stalks (cut into	2 tbs oyster sauce
small chunks)	
2 cloves of garlic, peeled and	
sliced	

Heat the oil in a wok until it smokes. Add the chicken of the woods and the broccoli and stir-fry for 2 minutes. Add the garlic and stir-fry for 1 minute longer. Add the sugar and salt. Stir and add the Shaohsing wine. Stir, add the water, turn heat to low, cover the wok and simmer for 3 more minutes. Remove the cover, increase the heat and add the oyster sauce. Toss to glaze and serve immediately.

Oyster mushrooms in oyster sauce

This is something of a culinary pun: oyster mushrooms only look like oysters, but oyster sauce really is made with them and, happily, their partnership is successful. Serves four as an accompaniment to many Chinese dishes providing they do not contain oyster sauce, and plain rice. Shaohsing wine and oyster sauce are available in oriental shops, but sherry and soy sauce may be substituted (as the latter is already salty, omit the salt).

3 tbs peanut oil
2 cloves of garlic, peeled and
  thinly sliced
white part of 4 spring
  onions, washed and sliced
  (reserve the sliced green
  leaves for a garnish)

450 g (1 lb) oyster
  mushrooms, cleaned and
  sliced
½ tsp salt
2 tbs Shaohsing wine
4 tbs oyster sauce

Heat a well-seasoned wok or deep pot and pour in the oil. When it starts to smoke, add the garlic and white sections of the spring onions. Toss them for 30 seconds before adding the mushrooms. Toss for 2 more minutes, then add the salt and Shaohsing wine. Let this partially evaporate and add the oyster sauce. Toss to coat, sprinkle with the green spring onion, and serve immediately.

Stir-fried mushrooms with lettuce

Serve this healthy and very attractive vegetable stir-fry with oriental fish, meat or poultry dishes, and plenty of plain boiled rice. Normally tasteless, iceberg lettuce has the right firm texture to withstand a brief exposure to heat, but you can use tastier hearts of Cos lettuce or 2–3 'Little Gem' lettuces. The carrots and purple skins of the aubergines give the dish colour.

3 tbs peanut oil
3 large carrots, scrubbed and
  very thinly sliced
225 g (8 oz) chestnut
  mushrooms, sliced
1 medium aubergine, in 2 cm
  (1 inch) cubes

4 cloves of garlic, peeled and
  thinly sliced
3 tbs Shaohsing wine
3 tbs oyster sauce
small iceberg lettuce, roughly
  shredded

Heat the oil to smoking point. Add the carrots and mushrooms and stir-fry for a minute. Add the aubergine and garlic and stir-fry for 2 minutes longer. Pour in the Shaohsing wine and mix well (it will evaporate quickly). Cover the wok, reduce the heat, and let the vegetables steam for 2–3 minutes, or until they are just tender. Stir in the oyster sauce and the lettuce. Transfer to a warm serving bowl and serve immediately.

Curried mushrooms

Serving two, these spicy mushrooms may accompany Indian dishes with plenty of boiled rice and a vegetable relish.

3 tbs peanut oil
1 tsp fennel seeds
225 g (8 oz) oyster and shiitake mushrooms, wiped and sliced
1 tsp coriander seeds, ground
1 tsp cumin seeds, ground
½ tsp turmeric
½ tsp cayenne pepper

3 cloves of garlic, peeled and chopped
small piece of fresh ginger, peeled and chopped
½ tsp salt
6 tbs water
juice of a lime or half a lemon
2 ripe tomatoes, peeled and chopped

Heat the oil in a wok or non-stick pan, throw in the fennel seeds and the mushrooms and toss for 1 minute. Add the ground coriander and cumin, turmeric, cayenne, garlic and ginger and mix well. Add the salt, water, citrus juice and tomato, increase the heat, and cook for 8 more minutes. Serve.

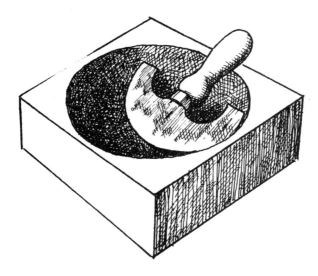

FISH, POULTRY, GAME AND MEAT

Red snapper and mushrooms baked en papillote

Whole, firm white-fleshed fish (or steaks or fillets) are baked in greaseproof paper or foil parcels, with herbs, olive oil, a little wine, mushrooms, and other vegetables. Other suitable fish include Mediterranean sea bream or grouper steaks. Serves four.

2 large (or 4 small) red
   snapper, or 4 fish steaks
salt
freshly milled black pepper
6 tbs olive oil, plus a little for
   wiping the foil or
   greaseproof paper
175 g (6 oz) button
   mushrooms, thickly sliced
2 cloves of garlic, peeled and
   chopped
1 small carrot, peeled and
   diced

4 shallots, peeled and
   chopped
2 potatoes, peeled and very
   thinly sliced
6 tbs tomato passata
generous handful of fresh
   parsley, washed and
   chopped
110 ml (4 fl oz) dry white
   wine
a little extra virgin olive oil
1 lemon, cut into quarters

Rinse the fish in running water and pat dry. Season inside and out, if whole, or on both sides, if steaks or fillets are used. Preheat the oven to 200°C/400°F/gas mark 6. Have ready individual rectangles of foil or greaseproof paper, large enough to enclose each portion. Wipe each one with olive oil.

Heat the remaining olive oil in a pan; gently fry the mushrooms for a few minutes until they have reduced and shed some liquid; add the garlic, carrot, shallots and potatoes and fry gently for 2 minutes longer. Season. Cover the pan, reduce the heat and simmer the vegetables until they have softened, stirring once or twice (about 4 more minutes). Add the tomato and cook, uncovered, for a further 2 or 3 minutes.

Remove from the heat. Divide the vegetables between the portions, spreading a layer on the oiled foil or paper. Arrange the fish on top, scatter liberally with parsley, season, and cover with another layer of vegetables. Pour over a little white wine and sprinkle with extra virgin olive oil (2–3 tsp per portion). Fold the parcels over tightly, to seal.

Bake in the oven until the fish is flaky (10 minutes for steaks, 15–20 minutes for whole fish). Serve, still tightly wrapped, on warm plates, and garnish with lemon wedges.

Salmon fillets with mushroom and mustard sauce

Salmon and mushrooms are not generally considered successful partners. However, the traditional, slightly sweet and sour Scandinavian mustard sauce that often accompanies gravadlax (marinated salmon) is very good. For that reason, I experimented by combining the sauce with mushrooms. Normally, the sauce is a cold emulsion but I discovered that it can also be the base of a very good hot mushroom sauce. Serves four with boiled potatoes.

Mustard sauce

3 tbs English mustard
  powder
1 tbs sugar
1 tbs white wine or cider
  vinegar
4 tbs sunflower oil
4 tbs soured cream or crème
  fraîche
fresh dill, washed and
  chopped

4 salmon fillets
freshly milled black pepper
4 tbs olive oil
50 g (2 oz) unsalted butter
350 g (12 oz) shiitake, oyster
  and chestnut mushrooms,
  trimmed and sliced
salt
freshly milled black pepper

Mix together the mustard sauce ingredients in a pot and reserve them. Place the salmon fillets on a plate and grind plenty of black pepper over them. Pour the olive oil over them.

Melt the butter in a pan with the mushrooms. Stir-fry over a medium heat for a minute, then reduce the heat and allow them to cook slowly until they have reduced in bulk and have acquired golden edges (this will take 8–12 minutes). Season and reserve.

Heat a dry non-stick frying pan and put in the salmon fillets. Cook for a minute on each side, then lower the heat and cook each side more gently until the fillets are lightly coloured but still moist within (the time required will depend upon the thickness but will not exceed 4 minutes for each side). Season the salmon with a little salt. While the salmon cooks, add the mushrooms to the sauce and heat, stirring well, until it has thickened. Serve on hot plates beside the salmon fillets.

Salmon steaks with mushroom sauce

These creamy sautéed button mushrooms, sharpened with lemon juice, complement the relatively assertive flavour of salmon. Farmed fish are acceptable but are usually rather bland. Serve with one of the more interesting varieties of boiling potatoes, such as Ratte, Charlotte, or Pink Fir Apple, and a vegetable. Serves four.

4 medium salmon steaks	*handful of fresh parsley*
freshly milled black pepper	*50 g (2 oz) butter*
2 tbs olive oil	*salt*
350 g (12 oz) button	*4 tbs lemon juice*
mushrooms	*6 tbs double cream*

Place the salmon steaks in a bowl. Season all over with black pepper and pour the olive oil over them. Turn them in the oil to coat; leave them while you prepare the remaining ingredients.

Wipe the mushrooms, trim off and discard the bottoms of the stems, and slice the mushrooms thickly. Wash the parsley, shake dry, and chop it finely.

Heat a well-seasoned or non-stick frying pan. Gently sauté the salmon fillets in the oil that clings to them, until all sides are pale gold (about 6 minutes). Remove, taking care not to break them, and transfer to a plate. In a separate pan melt the butter and add the mushrooms. Sauté for 3–4 minutes. Season with salt and freshly milled black pepper, add the lemon juice, and sauté for 4 more minutes, turning from time to time. Add the cream and parsley and mix well. Add the salmon, gently heat through and serve immediately.

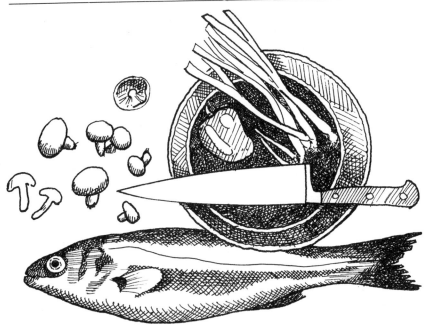

Steamed bass with mushrooms

I always include some thinly sliced oyster or button mushrooms when I steam a whole bass in the Cantonese manner. Serving four, this can be the centre-piece of an elegant dinner party, accompanied by plain rice and other oriental dishes, including some simple stir-fried vegetables in oyster sauce. Look for a fish weighing about ¾ kilo (1¾ lb).

1 medium striped bass or sea bass, gutted, cleaned and scaled
salt
freshly milled black pepper
2 cm (1 inch) piece of fresh ginger, peeled and finely chopped
4 spring onions, washed and thinly sliced

2 cloves of garlic, peeled and finely chopped
1 fresh green or red chilli, seeded and thinly sliced
110 g (4 oz) mushrooms, thinly sliced
5 tbs peanut oil
2 tsp Shaohsing wine
2 tsp sesame oil
2 tbs light soy sauce

Wash the fish in running water and pat it dry. Season it inside and out. Slash both sides diagonally two or three times with a sharp knife. If steaming in a wok, place the fish on a plate or platter, and stand that on a trivet. (If the fish is too big for the wok, trim off a large part of the tail with scissors, or cut the fish in two and lay the halves side by side on the plate.) Pour enough water into the wok to come up its sides but without reaching the plate.

Scatter the vegetables over and around the fish, bring the water to the boil, cover the wok, and steam until the flesh is flaky (about 10 minutes). Carefully pour off the excess water that will have condensed on the plate. Cover the wok again, without turning on the heat.

Heat the peanut oil in a small pan until it begins to smoke. Pour it over the fish to complete the cooking, and sprinkle with the Shaohsing wine, sesame oil and soy sauce. Your guests serve themselves by scooping up the flesh with a little of the sauce and the vegetables.

Petti di pollo alla boscaiola

'Alla boscaiola' refers to the woods and forests where wild mushrooms grow, and is frequently applied in Italian cooking to mushroom sauces, alluding to the simple cooking style of the forester. The dried ceps or morels and their soaking liquid add flavour. Serves four.

3 tbs extra virgin olive oil
4 large chicken breasts
225 g (8 oz) button mushrooms
1 stick of celery, finely sliced
2 cloves of garlic, peeled and chopped
handful of fresh parsley, washed and chopped

4 tbs dry white wine
salt
freshly milled black pepper
12 g (½ oz) reconstituted dried ceps or morels (allow 20 minutes to soak ceps, 30 for morels) and their strained soaking liquid
3 tinned tomatoes, chopped

Heat the oil in a pan and fry the chicken breasts until evenly golden. Remove them. Add the fresh mushrooms and celery and stir for 3–4 minutes. Add the garlic and parsley and stir around for 2 more minutes. Add the wine and cook over a high heat until it has evaporated. Season and add the dried mushrooms and their soaking liquid. Return the chicken to the pan. Add the tomatoes, stir and cover. Simmer for 20 minutes. Serve with rice or potatoes.

Braised chicken breasts with milk caps

This quick and easy recipe makes an ideal light lunch or supper for four people; other firm mushrooms can be used instead of the milk caps. It is imperative to retain the skins of the chicken breasts, which keep them moist.

225 g (8 oz) saffron milk
  caps or other firm
  mushrooms
4 tbs olive oil
4 free-range or corn-fed
  chicken breasts (skins left
  on)
sprigs of sage and rosemary
bay leaf

2 cloves of garlic, peeled and
  chopped
salt
freshly milled black pepper
200 g (7 oz) fresh or canned
  plum tomatoes, peeled and
  chopped
6 tbs white wine
12 stoned black olives

Clean the mushrooms; remove and discard the stems, and cut the caps into thick slices. Heat the oil in a large, well-seasoned frying pan. Fry the chicken breasts until golden on both sides. Remove and reserve them. Add the herbs, reduce the heat, and simmer them in the oil for 2–3 minutes. Add the mushrooms and garlic, and gently fry them for 3–4 minutes. Remove the herbs from the pan, return the chicken breasts, and season. Add the tomatoes and wine. Mix well, cover, and simmer for about 15 minutes. Add the olives and heat through. Serve with puréed potatoes and a green vegetable.

Chicken and mushroom involtini

These *involtini* (little rolls) cook very quickly; the effort that goes into making them, though scant, can be expended well in advance, and the dish finished after a few minutes' frying. Use thinly sliced fresh ceps, or replace these with chestnut mushrooms. Serves four with diced potatoes fried in olive oil with some fresh bay leaves, and broccoli or another vegetable.

3 corn-fed chicken breasts
110 g (4 oz) ceps or chestnut
  mushrooms
salt
freshly milled black pepper
75 g (3 oz) mozzarella, diced
  or cut into thin strips

4 tbs tomato passata
6–9 slices Parma or Bayonne
  ham
olive oil for frying

With a sharp knife, slice through the chicken breasts horizontally, making three large slices for very plump breasts or just two for smaller ones. Place the thin chicken slices between sheets of waxed paper or plastic and beat them with a few blows of a wooden mallet. (Do not over-flatten them or they will disintegrate: they should be thin but intact.)

Slice the mushrooms thinly. If using ceps, chop the slices into smaller pieces to fit on the chicken pieces.

Lay out the chicken on a board. Place a layer of mushrooms on each. Season. Sprinkle with mozzarella and top with a teaspoon of tomato. Roll up tightly and in turn wrap each piece tightly with the slices of ham.

Heat a layer of olive oil in a frying pan. Fry the involtini over a medium heat for just a couple of minutes on each side. (They will give off some liquid.) Serve while still very hot.

Braised chicken with dried ceps

Enriched with a little chicken stock, this delicious Italian braise is very simple and rewarding; better still, it can be prepared at any time of year with dried wild mushrooms. Serves four.

4 tbs olive oil
1 corn-fed chicken, cut into
serving pieces
1 small onion, peeled and
chopped
2 cloves of garlic, peeled and
chopped
25 g (1 oz) reconstituted
dried ceps and their
strained soaking liquid

pinch of thyme
6 tbs home-made chicken
stock (see recipe on p. 114)
200 g (7 oz) chopped tinned
tomatoes
salt
freshly milled black pepper

Heat the olive oil in a large pot; fry the chicken pieces until evenly golden. Remove and reserve them. Add the onions and fry them until translucent. Mix in the garlic. Return the chicken pieces, add the mushrooms and thyme, and moisten with stock, tomato and the mushrooms' soaking liquid. Season well, cover and simmer for 20 minutes. Reduce the liquid if necessary and serve with mashed potatoes.

Chicken with sherry and button mushrooms

Use very fresh, tight buttons which will turn juicy and delectable in this highly perfumed dish which is ideal for entertaining and serves four. You can also use larger buttons, halved. It is important to use a good quality fino sherry, which will impart a woody spiciness to the dish.

4 tbs *fruity olive oil*
1 *free-range or corn-fed*
   chicken, in small serving
   pieces
4 *slices of smoked back*
   bacon, trimmed and finely
   diced
1 *small onion, peeled and*
   finely chopped
350 g (12 oz) *button*
   mushrooms, stems
   trimmed, and caps wiped

4 *cloves of garlic, peeled and*
   chopped
zest and juice of ½ a lemon
4 tbs *fino sherry*
salt
freshly milled black pepper
generous handful of fresh
   parsley, washed and
   chopped

Heat the oil to smoking point in a heavy, lidded casserole. Fry the chicken pieces until evenly golden. Remove them with a slotted spoon and add the bacon and onion to the oil. Let them take on colour over a medium heat (about 3 minutes) before adding the mushrooms and garlic. Cook for 4 minutes, stirring often. Return the chicken to the casserole and pour in the lemon zest, juice and sherry. Season, cover and simmer for 15–20 minutes. Sprinkle with the parsley and serve with french fries, roast potatoes, or fried polenta.

Chicken with morels

A speciality of La Bresse, the part of southern Burgundy where the famed, eponymous *poulets* are bred. If using dried morels, which reconstitute perfectly, soak them in a small cup of hot water for half an hour. Serving four, this is delicious with an elegant rice pilaff, made with home-made chicken stock and saffron.

175 g (6 oz) fresh morels,
    halved vertically, and
    110 ml (4 fl oz) home-
    made chicken stock (see
    recipe on p. 114) or
    25 g (1 oz) dried morels
    and their strained soaking
    liquid
large corn-fed or free-range
    chicken

50 g (2 oz) butter
2 tbs olive oil
6 tbs brandy
6 tbs double cream
salt
freshly milled black pepper
a little chopped fresh parsley

Check the morels for dirt or sand; wash away all traces and pat them dry with kitchen paper. Cut the chicken into small serving pieces.

Melt the butter with the morels in a large, well-seasoned frying pan, adding the oil to prevent the butter from burning. Sauté them briefly, stirring all the while. Add the chicken pieces and gently fry them in the same pan until they are evenly golden, starting with the legs, which need longer cooking. Warm the brandy, pour into the pan and set it alight. Add the stock or the morels' soaking liquid (if using), cover the pan and simmer the chicken over a low heat for 25 minutes, turning the pieces a few times. (The sauce should not be too thin; reduce by boiling if necessary.) Add the cream, season, and heat through. Sprinkle with parsley, transfer to a warm serving dish and serve.

Poulet au vin

Here the long cooking time that is required to tenderize a barnyard cockerel has been reduced to suit the more tender roasting fowl that are readily available in our shops. The residual wine is reduced in the pot without the chicken, once it has cooked, because success is entirely dependent on the correct wine reduction.

large corn-fed or free-range
    chicken
4 tbs olive oil
1 carrot, scrubbed and diced
225 g (8 oz) small button
    mushrooms, whole

225 g (8 oz) pickling onions,
    peeled
1 small onion, peeled and
    chopped
2 cloves of garlic, peeled and
    finely chopped

pinch of dried thyme
2 bay leaves
560 ml (1 pint) red wine
salt

freshly milled black pepper
handful of fresh parsley,
    washed and chopped

Joint the chicken. Heat the oil in a heavy lidded casserole. Fry the chicken pieces until evenly golden. Add the carrots, mushrooms, pickling onions, chopped onion, garlic and herbs. Mix well, and allow the mushrooms to reduce a little. Pour in the wine and season. Simmer, uncovered, for 25–30 minutes. Remove and reserve the chicken pieces. Raise the heat and reduce the wine for about 20 minutes, by which time it should have become a luscious, rich sauce. Return the chicken and heat through. Sprinkle with parsley and serve at once with boiled new potatoes.

Roast chicken stuffed with mushrooms and pine nuts

Mushrooms and pine nuts are an excellent stuffing mixture for roast poultry. The mushrooms remain juicy and acquire a deeper flavour. Serves four with large croûtons or roast potatoes and some green beans.

2 tbs olive oil
5 shallots, peeled and
    chopped
225 g (8 oz) chestnut and
    shiitake mushrooms,
    halved
50 g (2 oz) pine nuts
4 cloves of garlic, peeled and
    chopped
salt
freshly milled black pepper

leaves of 3–4 sprigs of
    parsley, washed and
    chopped
1 large corn-fed chicken
2 bay leaves
4 tbs olive oil
4 tbs dry white wine
4 thick slices of French bread
4 tbs brandy
salt

Preheat the oven to 200°C/400°F/gas mark 6.

Heat 2 tablespoons of olive oil in a small pan; fry the shallots for a minute, then add the mushrooms and stir-fry for 3–4 minutes. Add the pine nuts and garlic, reduce the heat, and cook for 2–3 minutes longer. Season and mix in the parsley. Reserve.

Season the chicken all over with black pepper, including the cavity. Stuff with the mushroom mixture, and push in the bay leaves. Transfer the chicken to a roasting tin. Pour the olive oil and wine over the chicken. Roast for 30 minutes, basting occasionally. Turn, and roast the chicken for 20 more minutes, basting a few more times. Turn again and continue to roast for 10–15 more minutes, or until the skin is evenly crisp and golden. Put the bread in the oven for the last 5 minutes of roasting. Remove the chicken and let it rest on a board while you make the gravy: pour the roasting juices into a small pan, add the brandy, and reduce quickly to a dense sauce. Meanwhile, sprinkle the chicken with salt; joint or carve it. Spoon the stuffing onto the baked slices of bread and serve with the gravy.

Chicken in coconut milk with shiitake

This delicious curry with shiitake mushrooms serves two with plenty of boiled rice and a stir-fried vegetable. All the ingredients are readily available in oriental shops and larger supermarkets.

4 tbs peanut oil	1 tsp sugar
4 cloves of garlic, peeled and thinly sliced	1 tsp salt
	½ tsp cayenne pepper
2 cm (1 inch) piece of fresh ginger, peeled and finely chopped	1 tbs Thai fish sauce or soy sauce
	1 tbs good quality curry paste (see recipe on p. 52 for home-made 'red' curry paste)
110 g (4 oz) fresh shiitake mushrooms, trimmed and thickly sliced	
2 red chillies, seeded and sliced from top to bottom	200 ml (7 fl oz) tinned coconut milk
225 g (8 oz) chicken breasts, skinned and cubed	110 g (4 oz) bean sprouts
	handful of fresh basil leaves

Heat the oil in the wok to smoking point. Add the garlic and ginger. Stir. Add the mushrooms and chillies and stir them around for 1 minute. Add the chicken and stir-fry until all the pieces turn white (about 1 minute). Now add the sugar, salt, cayenne pepper and fish or soy sauce and stir well. Stir in the curry paste and fry with the other ingredients for another minute. Pour in the coconut milk and boil until it thickens and darkens, and the oil begins to separate from the sauce. Add the bean sprouts and cook for 30 seconds longer. Sprinkle with the basil and serve at once.

Braised guinea fowl with wild mushrooms

As is so often the case, wild mushrooms can be replaced by a mixture of cultivated mushrooms and dried ceps, soaked and reconstituted in warm water. Although guinea fowl has a slightly gamier flavour, a whole cleaned chicken (preferably free-range or corn-fed) can be cooked in exactly the same way. Serves four.

4 tbs olive oil
2 small cleaned guinea fowl
1 large onion, peeled and
    coarsely chopped
sprigs of rosemary and sage
bay leaf
1 carrot, scrubbed and finely
    chopped
2 cloves of garlic, peeled and
    chopped
225 g (8 oz) wild
    mushrooms, cleaned and
    sliced or 225 g (8 oz)

cultivated mushrooms,
    sliced, and 12 g (½ oz)
    reconstituted dried ceps
    and their strained soaking
    liquid
225 ml (8 fl oz) dry white
    wine
1 tbs tomato purée
salt
freshly milled black pepper

Choose a very large, heavy, lidded pot with steep sides that will accommodate the fowl. Heat the olive oil and gently fry the fowl until golden all over. Remove and reserve them. Sauté the onion in the same oil until lightly coloured. Add the herbs, carrot and garlic. Mix well. Add the fresh mushrooms, and the drained ceps (if using); gently fry for 3–4 minutes. (If using dried ceps, add their soaking liquid now and allow it to evaporate.) Add the wine and tomato purée, season, and mix well. Return the fowl to the pot; spoon the sauce over them, cover, and simmer for 45 minutes – prod them to check that the flesh is tender – turning several times and basting with the sauce. Remove the rosemary, sage and bay leaf and serve, jointed, with the sauce.

Casseroled pheasant

The gamey flavour of pheasant needs fairly robust ingredients such as smoked bacon, celery and wild mushrooms. Use mixed wild mushrooms, or a combination of dried ceps and cultivated shiitake, oyster and button mushrooms. One bird serves two. (Serve the breasts but keep the rather tough legs and the carcass to make game stock or soup.)

cleaned pheasant
freshly milled black pepper
4 tbs olive oil
small onion, peeled and
   chopped
stick of celery, thinly sliced
2 slices of smoked bacon,
   trimmed and diced
2 cloves of garlic, peeled and
   chopped
2 bay leaves
225 g (8 oz) wild
   mushrooms, cleaned and
   sliced or 225 g (8 oz)

cultivated mushrooms,
cleaned and sliced, and
12 g (½ oz) reconstituted
dried ceps and their
strained soaking liquid
225 ml (8 fl oz) white wine
salt
handful of fresh parsley,
   washed and chopped

Season the pheasant generously all over with black pepper. Heat the olive oil to smoking point in a large casserole. Brown the bird all over, then remove and reserve it.

Add the onion, celery, bacon, garlic and bay leaves to the casserole, reduce the heat to medium, and gently fry for about 3 minutes or until the vegetables and the bacon are lightly coloured. Add the mushrooms and stir them with the vegetables until they have reduced in bulk (about 4 minutes). Return the pheasant to the casserole. (If using dried ceps, add their soaking liquid now and allow it to evaporate.) Pour in the wine, season, mix well, and cover.

Reduce the heat and simmer until tender (about an hour), turning a few times. A few minutes before the pheasant is ready, check the sauce; remove the cover and reduce the liquid, if necessary. Sprinkle with the parsley and serve the breasts with the sauce and puréed potatoes or polenta.

Catalan rabbit casserole with mushrooms

Catalans usually thicken their stews and casseroles with *picadas*, aromatic pastes of hazelnuts, pine nuts or almonds, pounded with fresh herbs and garlic, which are added towards the end of the cooking time to impart fragrance. The basic recipe also works with a whole roasting chicken and with beef or veal (if the latter, use about 675 g (1½ lb), add a little water to the cooking liquid, and simmer until tender). Serves four.

4 tbs olive oil
1 kg (2¼ lb) skinned and
   jointed rabbit

large onion, peeled and
   chopped
large carrot, peeled and diced

2 sticks of celery, diced
350 g (12 oz) closed-cap
  button mushrooms, halved
  or quartered if large
2 tbs tomato purée

225 ml (8 fl oz) white wine
4 tbs dry sherry
salt
freshly milled black pepper

Picada

2 cloves of garlic, peeled
50 g (2 oz) hazelnuts
  (shelled weight)
4 sprigs of flat-leaved
  parsley, washed

2 tbs extra virgin olive oil
pinch of salt

Heat the olive oil in a large, lidded casserole. Brown the rabbit pieces evenly. Transfer them to a plate.

Fry the onion, carrot and celery in the oil until pale golden. Add the mushrooms and stir-fry for 3–4 minutes. Return the rabbit pieces, add the tomato purée, pour in the wine and sherry, season, and bring to the boil. Reduce the heat, cover, and simmer for 35 minutes.

Meanwhile, pound the *picada* ingredients to a paste with a pestle and mortar, mixing in the oil when the nuts are crushed (or grind everything to a paste in a food processor). Add to the casserole and continue to simmer for 10 more minutes. Serve with potatoes and a vegetable.

Venison medallions with wild mushrooms

Venison, though increasingly fashionable, is relatively undervalued in Britain. Available from game dealers and occasionally in supermarkets, venison benefits from a period of marination. There is no better accompaniment than wild mushrooms, with which it shares the autumnal season. Here, the mushrooms are cooked in the venison's strained marinade. Serves two.

Marinade

2 venison medallions, from
  the fillet
small onion, peeled and
  quartered
bay leaf
pinch of dried thyme

small piece of cinnamon
2 tsp juniper berries
plenty of freshly milled black
  pepper
6 tbs tawny port or Madeira
3 tbs fruity olive oil

Trim the venison of all visible fat and discard it. Put the trimmed fillets in a bowl and combine with the marinade ingredients. Cover and refrigerate. Leave overnight and preferably for 24 hours.

Remove the venison and sprinkle more black pepper over it. Strain and reserve the marinade.

225 g (8 oz) wild
  mushrooms, cleaned and
  sliced (if large) or
225 g (8 oz) cultivated
  shiitake and oyster
  mushrooms and
12 g (½ oz) reconstituted
  dried ceps and their
  strained soaking liquid

40 g (1½ oz) butter
salt
freshly milled black pepper
2 tbs olive oil
4 tbs tawny port or Madeira
12 g (½ oz) butter
fresh parsley, washed and
  chopped

Stir-fry the mushrooms in the butter for 2–3 minutes. Season, reduce the heat and continue to cook more gently for 3 more minutes. Add the strained marinade (and the mushrooms' soaking liquid, if using), raise the heat and allow the sauce to thicken. Remove from the heat before all the liquid has evaporated.

Meanwhile, heat the olive oil to smoking point in a small, non-stick pan. Quickly sear the venison on both sides, reduce the heat and cook each side for a few minutes longer. Deglaze the pan with a little tawny port or Madeira and enrich the mushrooms with the pan juices, butter and a sprinkling of parsley. Serve the venison with the mushrooms, some potatoes and redcurrant jelly.

Marinated loin of lamb with morels

Best with fresh morels and wonderful, tender new season's lamb, this delicious, spring-time dish serves four and needs no other accompaniment. It can also be made with reconstituted dried morels.

Marinade

800 g (1¾ lb) loin of lamb
2 cloves of garlic, peeled and
  crushed
225 ml (8 fl oz) extra virgin
  olive oil

juice of a lemon
pinch of dried oregano
bay leaf
freshly milled black pepper

Trim the lamb and cut it into cubes each about 2 cm (1 inch) square. Put them in a bowl with the crushed garlic. Stir in the olive oil and lemon juice; add the herbs and sprinkle generously with black pepper. Mix well, cover and set aside for at least two hours.

Morels

175 g (6 oz) fresh morels or
   25 g (1 oz) dried morels
medium onion, peeled and
   chopped
3 tbs olive oil
675 g (1½ lb) potatoes,
   peeled and diced small
110 ml (4 fl oz) home-made
   vegetable stock (see recipe
   on p. 114) or the morels'
   soaking liquid

2 tbs tomato passata
salt
freshly milled black pepper
handful of fresh parsley,
   washed and chopped

Wash the morels thoroughly and drain them well. (If using dried morels reconstitute them in hot water for 30 minutes. Strain and reserve their soaking liquid.) Soften the onion in the olive oil, but do not allow to brown. Add the morels and the potatoes to the pan, raise the heat and fry for 2–3 minutes. Reduce the heat and continue to stir-fry for 3–4 minutes longer. Pour in the stock (or the morels' soaking liquid), and the passata. Season, cover and simmer until the potatoes are tender. Sprinkle with parsley and reserve.

Preheat a grill or cast-iron griddle. Remove the lamb from the marinade and thread it onto skewers. Cook for 3–4 minutes on each side. Meanwhile, reheat the morels. Sprinkle the lamb with salt and serve at once with the morels.

Loin of pork with mushrooms and madeira

Pork loin is an excellent, tender cut that needs only 10 minutes' cooking. Not only are these medallions perfectly delicious, they are also easy to cook. Serves two.

275–350 g (10–12 oz) pork
   loin, trimmed
freshly milled black pepper
25 g (1 oz) butter
1 tbs olive oil
225 g (8 oz) button
   mushrooms, wiped clean
   and thinly sliced

1 clove of garlic, peeled and
   chopped
salt
140 ml (5 fl oz) Madeira
2 tbs crème fraîche
fresh parsley, washed and
   chopped

Cut the pork into medallions about 3 cm (1¼ inches) thick. Season them all over very generously with black pepper. Heat the butter and oil in a well-seasoned or non-stick frying pan and fry the pork gently until golden all over (about 10 minutes). Remove and reserve it. Add the mushrooms to the pan, raise the heat and stir-fry for 3–4 minutes. Add the garlic, mix well and season with salt. Pour in the Madeira and let it thicken. Return the pork, stir in the crème fraîche and heat through. Sprinkle with parsley and serve with boiled new potatoes and a cooked vegetable.

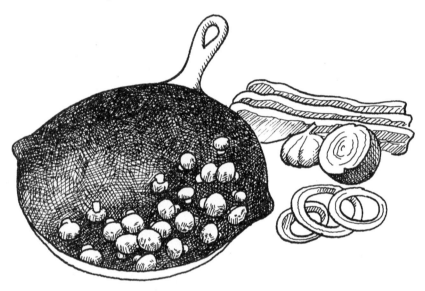

Marinated strips of veal or beef with mushrooms

Ingredients typically found in an Italian kitchen are treated here in an oriental way, rapidly fried after a period of marination to flavour the meat, and enhanced by the bacon, mushrooms and olives. Serves four with puréed potatoes or celeriac, mashed cannellini beans, or fennel bulbs braised in olive oil, with parmesan.

575 g (1¼ lb) veal escalopes, or beef tenderloin or rump
225 ml (8 fl oz) olive oil
1 onion, peeled and roughly chopped
2 cloves of garlic, peeled
2 tbs dry sherry or dry vermouth

freshly milled black pepper
3 slices of bacon
110 g (4 oz) button mushrooms, halved or quartered
140 ml (5 fl oz) dry white wine
16 pitted green olives

Slice the veal or beef into strips 2 cm (1 inch) wide and ½ cm (¼ inch) thick, and put them in a bowl.

Prepare the marinade by adding two-thirds of the olive oil, half the chopped onion, 1 chopped clove of garlic, the sherry or vermouth, and black pepper. Mix well, cover and leave for at least an hour, preferably longer.

Finely chop the other garlic clove. Trim the bacon and cut it into small strips. Heat a heavy frying pan and add the remaining olive oil, then add the bacon, remaining onion and garlic and sauté until soft, without burning. Add the mushrooms and mix well.

Meanwhile, heat a smaller non-stick frying pan and rapidly seal the meat in the oil that will still cling to it from the marinade. Do this in batches so as not to overcrowd the pan. When the meat has all been sealed, transfer it to the pan containing the mushrooms. Deglaze the other pan with the wine, loosening any scraps. When bubbling, pour the winey juice over the main ingredients and continue to cook until the sauce is thick and the wine has all but evaporated, about 3 more minutes. Add the olives and heat through. Transfer to a heated serving dish, the meat to one side and the accompanying vegetables to the other.

Steaks with wild mushroom sauce

This is a favourite Sunday lunch which I always cook in October with my booty of fresh ceps from the boskier parts of Wimbledon Common, and which we continue to enjoy in the winter months with the trusty combination of cultivated mushrooms and dried ceps. Serves four.

4 rump or fillet steaks
freshly milled black pepper
6 tbs olive oil
75 g (3 oz) unsalted butter
6 shallots, peeled and
   chopped
175 g (6 oz) fresh ceps,
   trimmed and sliced, and
   110 ml (4 fl oz) stock or
   175 g (6 oz) cultivated
   mushrooms, trimmed and
   sliced, and 25 g (1 oz)
   reconstituted dried ceps
   and their strained soaking
   liquid

1 tbs tomato purée
salt
freshly milled black pepper
110 ml (4 fl oz) white wine
6 tbs tawny port

Sprinkle the steaks with plenty of black pepper and pour 4 tbs of the olive oil over them. Reserve them.

Heat the remaining olive oil and half of the butter in a pan with the shallots. Sauté them until they begin to colour. Add the fresh mushrooms and sauté them for about 5 minutes. Add the stock, or the reconstituted ceps and their soaking liquid; add the tomato purée, and reduce to a very thick sauce. Season, then add the wine and port. Reduce by two thirds.

Meanwhile, cook the steaks under the grill or on a very hot griddle or dry pan, seasoning them with salt only when they are done. Add the remaining butter to the mushroom sauce and heat through. Serve the steaks with the mushroom sauce and some french fries or sautéed potatoes.

Beef stroganoff

I hesitated to include a recipe for beef stroganoff because it is so familiar. I concluded, however, that a classic dish such as this should not be ignored. The problem so often is inferior beef. Unless it has been properly hung and is sweet and really tender, the dish will at best be mediocre. (Alas, you are unlikely to find beef of that quality in a supermarket.) The dish is named after Alexander Stroganov, a Russian aristocrat whose chef created it to serve to the many guests Stroganov entertained at his seaside home in Odessa. Serves six, with rice.

450 g (1 lb) fillet of beef
freshly milled black pepper
75 g (3 oz) butter
1 large onion, peeled and
  very finely chopped
225 g (8 oz) button
  mushrooms, thinly sliced
salt
small pinch of freshly ground
  nutmeg

small pinch of cayenne
  pepper
1 tbs tomato passata
4 tbs white wine
175 ml (6 fl oz) double
  cream, soured with the
  juice of half a lemon

Trim the beef of fat and cut it into thin slices. Cut them into narrow strips and season thoroughly with black pepper. Melt half of the butter in a non-stick frying pan; fry the onions and the mushrooms gently for about 4 minutes. Season with salt, a light grating of nutmeg and cayenne pepper. Add the tomato and wine, mix and cook for 2 more minutes; reserve. In another pan, stir-fry the beef for just 1 minute in the remaining butter.

Season the beef with salt. Add it and its pan juices to the sauce, mixing well. Add the soured cream and heat through, without boiling. Serve with pilaff or boiled rice.

Fillet of beef with mushrooms

This opulent and elegant dish serves two and is ideal to celebrate a special occasion. (Double the quantities to entertain four people, but remember that a larger piece of fillet needs a longer cooking time.) When available, by all means substitute any firm wild mushrooms.

25 g (1 oz) butter
1 tbs olive oil
350 g (12 oz) piece of beef
*   fillet, trimmed*
2 shallots, peeled and
*   chopped*
1 clove of garlic
small piece of cinnamon

225 g (8 oz) chestnut
*   mushrooms, sliced*
salt
freshly milled black pepper
6 tbs white wine
a little fresh parsley, washed
*   and chopped*
3 tbs double cream

Melt the butter in a pan with the olive oil. Gently brown the beef on all sides, remove and reserve it. (A 350 g (12 oz) piece will take 6–8 minutes, cooked rare to medium rare.)

Sauté the shallots, garlic and cinnamon in the fat for 2 minutes. Add the mushrooms, season well and fry gently for about 5 minutes, stirring all the time. Pour in the wine, increase the heat to maximum, and reduce the liquid to a thickish sauce. Reduce the heat, return the beef to the pan, sprinkle with parsley, add the cream and heat through for a couple of minutes. Slice the beef into two equal portions, and serve on warm plates.

Marinated beef fillet with wild mushrooms

Tender beef fillet goes very well with wild mushrooms, especially ceps. A marinade of onion, fresh herbs and Madeira or tawny port flavours the beef; this marinade is strained and reduced with the mushrooms. Serves two.

275–350 g (10–12 oz) piece
  of beef fillet, trimmed
4 tbs Madeira or tawny port
6 tbs dry white wine
3 tbs extra virgin olive oil
freshly milled black pepper
bay leaf
pinch of dried thyme
medium onion, peeled and
  chopped

olive oil, for frying
salt
25 g (1 oz) butter
225 g (8 oz) cleaned, sliced
  wild mushrooms
  (preferably ceps) or mixed
  cultivated mushrooms
salt
handful of fresh parsley,
  washed and chopped

Marinate the beef for several hours with the wines, extra virgin olive oil, black pepper, herbs and onion. Lift the beef from the marinade, straining and reserving the latter. Pat the beef dry.

Heat the remaining olive oil in a non-stick frying pan and seal the beef all over. Reduce the heat and cook for 7–8 minutes (medium rare), or for a few minutes longer for well-done beef. Sprinkle the beef with a little salt just before serving.

Meanwhile, melt the butter in a separate pan. Add the mushrooms and gently fry them for about 6 minutes. Add the strained marinade, season with salt and freshly milled black pepper, and raise the heat. Reduce the liquid to a fairly thick sauce. Slice the beef into two equal portions, surround each with half the mushrooms in their sauce, sprinkle with fresh parsley, and serve with potatoes and a vegetable.

Filet de bœuf en croûte

Use good quality, properly hung beef to guarantee tenderness and a sweet flavour. The pastry is flavoured with a combination of dried wild and fresh cultivated mushrooms, cooked with a little cognac. Serves four.

575 g (1¼ lb) piece of beef
  fillet, trimmed
freshly milled black pepper
6 tbs olive oil
225 g (8 oz) oyster, shiitake
  and button mushrooms,
  sliced
12 g (½ oz) reconstituted
  dried ceps, chopped, and
  their strained soaking
  liquid

salt
pinch of dried thyme
4 tbs cognac or calvados
225 g (8 oz) puff pastry
  (thawed, if frozen)
milk
1 egg, beaten

Sprinkle the beef with black pepper. Heat half of the olive oil in a non-stick frying pan and sear the beef quickly on all sides, to seal it. Reserve.

Heat the remaining olive oil in another pan. Sauté the fresh and reconstituted mushrooms over a medium heat for 4 minutes. Season with salt and freshly milled black pepper, add the thyme, mix well, and gently fry for a minute longer. Add the soaking liquid and 2 tablespoons of cognac, and allow most of the liquid to evaporate. Set aside. Preheat the oven to 200°C/400°F/gas mark 6.

Divide the pastry into two equal balls. Apply a little flour to a working surface, and to the surface of a rolling pin. Roll out the balls into thin sheets. Coat one sheet with half of the mushroom mixture. Lightly salt the beef all over, and place it over the mushroom-coated sheet of pastry. Cover the beef with the remaining mushroom mixture, then lay the other pastry sheet over that. Pinch the overlapping edges together, and moisten them with milk, to seal. Brush the pastry surfaces with the beaten egg. Pierce the pastry repeatedly with a fork, and make a small hole at the top. Roast for about 10 minutes, then introduce the remaining cognac through the hole, and roast for 5–10 minutes longer. (The beef should have a pink and juicy centre.) Serve very hot, with roast potatoes and a vegetable.

Steak, mushroom and stout pie

This hearty pie can be made with ready-made puff or shortcrust pastry. Browns restaurant in Oxford used to make a similar pie with a huge, risen puff pastry lid – a great favourite of mine and many of my friends when we were students there. This recipe makes a pie large enough for four.

675 g (1½ lb) braising
  steak, trimmed and cubed
a little flour, seasoned with
  freshly milled black pepper
4 tbs olive oil
3 slices of lean bacon,
  trimmed and diced
1 large onion, peeled and
  chopped
1 carrot, scrubbed and diced
small piece of cinnamon
450 g (1 lb) chestnut
  mushrooms, cleaned and
  halved

450 ml (¾ pint) stout
2 cloves of garlic, peeled and
  chopped
2 bay leaves
2 tbs tomato purée
salt
freshly milled black pepper
350 g (12 oz) puff or
  shortcrust pastry (thawed,
  if frozen)
milk or beaten egg

Roll the beef in the seasoned flour, to coat. Heat the olive oil to smoking point in a heavy, lidded casserole. Brown the beef on all sides in batches. Remove and transfer the beef to a platter. Fry the bacon just long enough to remove the rawness, then fry the onion, carrot and cinnamon more gently until they have softened and coloured slightly. Sauté the mushrooms for about a minute, then deglaze the pan with just a little stout (keep about 280 ml (½ pint)). Stir the mushrooms in the liquid while it evaporates. Remove the cinnamon, return the beef to the casserole and mix in the garlic and bay leaves. Pour in the remaining stout and stir in the tomato purée. Season, cover and simmer for 1½–1¾ hours. The sauce should be thick, dark and luscious, and the beef tender.

Preheat the oven to 200°C/400°F/gas mark 6. Roll out the pastry on a floured work surface. Cut a long strip that will fit around the rim of a deep pie dish. Moisten the rim of the pie dish and press the pastry strip on to it. Cut a lid out of the dough, reserving the scraps to make leaf decorations. Pile the cooked pie filling into the dish. Moisten the pastry rim. Fit the lid to the rim and press them together, to seal the pie. Decorate the lid with the scraps of pastry, brush with beaten egg or milk and bake until golden (20 minutes). Reduce the oven temperature to 180°C/350°F/gas mark 4 and continue to bake for 10 more minutes. Serve very hot, with a salad or cooked vegetables.

Bœuf bourgignon

Like other great regional dishes that have travelled well, this classic Burgundian beef stew is too often a travesty of the real thing. Here is an excellent, authentic recipe, serving six, in which the beef marinates first in red wine.

1 kg (2¼ lb) piece of stewing beef (tail end of rump, or chump)
1 bottle of red wine
2–3 sprigs of fresh thyme (or a pinch of dried)
2 bay leaves
2–3 sprigs of fresh parsley
1 medium onion, peeled and sliced
6 tbs olive oil
2 shallots, peeled and chopped
1 carrot, scrubbed and diced
2 cloves of garlic, peeled and finely chopped
salt
freshly milled black pepper
6 slices of back bacon, trimmed and diced
12–16 pickling or other small onions (depending on size), peeled
225 g (8 oz) button mushrooms, halved if large

Trim the beef. Cut it into evenly sized cubes, each about 3 cm (1½ inches) square. Marinate with the wine, herbs and onion in a large enamelled, glass or earthenware pot for at least 12 and up to 24 hours. Lift the beef from the marinade and drain well. Strain the marinade, discarding the solids.

Heat 4 tablespoons of the olive oil in a heavy lidded casserole. Brown the beef in batches and reserve. Add the shallots and the carrot to fry until golden, then add the garlic and mix well. Return the beef, season well, and pour in the strained wine from the marinade. Bring to the boil, cover and simmer very gently on the hob for 2½ hours. Meanwhile, heat the remaining oil in a small non-stick frying pan. Fry the bacon until just crisp, remove with a slotted spoon and add to the casserole. Reheat the oil and lightly brown the onions. Reserve them, and add to the casserole for the final hour of cooking. About 25 minutes before serving, add the mushrooms (and leave off the lid if the stew is too thin, to thicken). Serve with roasted or sautéed potatoes.

Daube of beef with mushrooms

This is a hearty beef stew to enjoy in the depths of winter when only cultivated mushrooms are available. Choose good quality stewing cuts of beef – the tail end of rump is ideal. Serves four with baked or boiled potatoes. This can be prepared in advance up to the point of adding the mushrooms; indeed, the flavour improves when the daube is served the following day.

4 tbs olive oil	salt
1 kg (2¼ lb) beef, trimmed and cut into 4 cm (2½ inch) cubes	freshly milled black pepper
	1 heaped tbs tomato purée
	350 ml (12 fl oz) red wine
2 onions, peeled and chopped	6 tbs water
1 carrot, scrubbed and chopped	piece of orange peel
	2 bay leaves
1 stick of celery, trimmed and sliced	2–3 sprigs of thyme or a pinch of dried thyme
4 cloves of garlic, peeled and chopped	225 g (8 oz) button mushrooms, left whole

Heat the oil in a heavy pot. Brown the beef chunks evenly in batches and reserve. Brown the onions, add the carrot and celery and fry for 2 minutes longer. Add the garlic, mix well, and return the beef. Season, add the tomato purée, wine, water, orange peel and herbs. Mix well. Cover, reduce the heat to minimum and simmer very gently for 2 hours, stirring occasionally. Add the mushrooms, cover and simmer for 15 minutes longer. Remove the thyme stalks and bay leaves and serve.

PRESERVES AND MISCELLANEA

Pickled mushrooms

Use this recipe to preserve firm mushrooms in good condition, whether wild or cultivated, sliced or whole. Slimy, damaged or elderly specimens are unsuitable. The method works as well with mixed as with single varieties; indeed, a pickling jar filled with different mushrooms looks very attractive. Italians, Poles and Russians make the most of the autumn crops by pickling any mushrooms that are surplus to immediate eating requirements, for later enjoyment throughout the winter months. Preserved with pickling spices to counteract the tart vinegar, they are excellent served in smallish portions with charcuterie, or as an antipasto to accompany a selection of little delicacies. You can substitute other herbs and spices and add peeled garlic cloves. You will need one large glass jar with a tight-fitting lid (pickling jars are ideal), or two small ones. The mushrooms should keep for many months, providing all your equipment is sterile.

900 g (2 lbs) mushrooms	*6 cloves*
560 ml (1 pint) each of	*1 tsp black peppercorns*
wine vinegar and water	*1 tsp coriander seeds*
1 tbs salt	*some large, dried red chillies*
3 bay leaves	*olive oil to fill the pickling jar*

First clean and trim the mushrooms, rejecting any that are bruised or blemished. Slice or leave them whole, depending upon their size. Put them in a large pot with all the remaining ingredients except the olive oil. Mix well while you bring the liquid to a boil. Cover and simmer them for about 8 minutes. Drain, manipulating them only with implements that have been sterilized in very freshly boiled water, and allow the mushrooms to cool. While they are cooling, sterilize a large glass pickling jar in the same way, and drain it well. Spoon in the mushrooms and the pickling herbs and spices. Fill the jar with olive oil, stirring to release any trapped air bubbles. There should be a generous layer of olive oil over the mushrooms. Seal and leave the mushrooms for a few weeks.

Russian marinated mushrooms

This traditional Russian method of preserving mushrooms differs from the conventional pickling method in that the fungi are marinated in pickling solution, having first simmered in salted water. Use only to preserve *firm* varieties of wild or cultivated mushrooms, whether they are mixed or of a single variety.

1¾ litres (3 pints) water	4 cloves
1 tbs salt	1 tsp salt
900 g (2 lb) wild or	1 tsp juniper berries
cultivated mushrooms,	1 tsp black peppercorns
sliced or left whole	1 tsp caraway seeds
according to size	6 fronds of fresh dill
175 ml (6 fl oz) white wine	sunflower oil (or other
or cider vinegar	vegetable oil) to fill the
110 ml (4 fl oz) water	pickling jar

Bring the salted water to the boil in a large pot and immerse the mushrooms. Return to the boil, cover and simmer them for about 6 minutes. Drain them well (use a sterilized slotted spoon) and, once they have cooled a little, transfer them to a large, sterile pickling jar. Bring the remaining ingredients except the oil to a simmer in a separate pan and cook for 3 minutes. Allow the liquid to cool and pour it over the mushrooms. Top up with the oil, to give a generous covering, and seal tightly. Leave for a month before using.

Porcini oil

Oils flavoured with porcini mushrooms and, best of all, truffles can be bought in some Italian delicatessens, but they can be prohibitively expensive. White truffle oil is best. You can make your own by infusing dried ceps in good quality olive oil for a month or more, then, if you like, straining the oil into a clean bottle. Little bottles of porcini oil make perfect gifts if attractively packaged and presented. You could use small jars with little pouring spouts or the attractive glass containers in which luxury ingredients such as balsamic vinegar are sometimes sold, but clean them well first. Tie a red ribbon around the neck of the jar for a special festive note and, if you have lost the lid and the neck is sufficiently narrow, stop with a clean cork and seal with melted wax from a red candle.

12 g (½ oz) of dried porcini mushrooms will impart a delicious aroma to a small quantity – say 170 ml (6 fl oz) of oil. You can use blended olive oil but extra virgin oil is more opulent, as befits the luxury of the flavouring ingredient. When the aroma is unmistakably mushroomy, the oil is ready for use. A trickle of porcini oil is excellent on crostini and bruschette, as well as in salads, soups, pasta dishes and risotti, not to mention on grilled or roasted fresh ceps.

Mushroom duxelles

Finely chopped mushrooms, sautéed to a fairly dry paste in butter with shallots, seasoning and fresh herbs can be added to stuffings, stirred into soups and white sauces, or used to line pastry, especially for beef *en croûte*. Duxelles may also be combined with poultry or game in pies, or used as a base for more elaborate mushroom preparations. I use them as the mushroom base for Polish pearl barley soup (see recipe on p. 76). Once cooked, the duxelles may be refrigerated for a few days or frozen.

50 g (2 oz) butter	*salt*
2–3 shallots, peeled and	*freshly milled black pepper*
finely chopped	*handful of fresh parsley,*
450 g (1 lb) cleaned and	*washed and chopped*
finely chopped mushrooms	

Melt the butter in a pan with the shallots. Let them colour slightly, then add the mushrooms. Season and fry them – initially over a fierce heat, then more gently – until they have reduced to a dense, dryish consistency. This will take about 20 minutes (or a little longer if the mushrooms are less than absolutely fresh and exude a lot of moisture). Stir in the parsley. Use straight away, or divide the duxelles into several equal portions and refrigerate or freeze in individual freezer bags.

Preserving mushrooms by drying and freezing

Several species of wild mushrooms are suitable for drying if they are picked reasonably dry (never sodden), especially ceps, bay boletus, horse mushrooms, cauliflower fungus, chanterelles, fairy ring mushrooms and morels. The first three should be sliced thinly, while cauliflower fungus should be pulled or cut into smallish chunks; chanterelles, fairy ring mushrooms and morels should be left whole. To dry properly, they should be placed on sheets of newspaper in a very warm, airy place. Turn the pieces over from time to time. Some people string them and hang them up to dry in garlands. Others recommend a cool fan oven with the door left ajar but I find this method unreliable as the mushrooms cook. Sunny window sills or the ledge above a central-heating boiler are good places to dry mushrooms. Only when they are absolutely dry and brittle should they be stored in jars or bags because any that have not dried out completely will spoil. Reconstitute up to 25 g (1 oz) at a time by soaking in a cup of hot water. Strain the soaking liquid and add it to the dish, as it will be intensely flavoured.

Firm young ceps, bay boleti and orange birch boleti can be frozen whole. Others can be cleaned, chopped or sliced, and sautéed in butter, then allowed to cool and frozen in food bags. Rapid defrosting is necessary for mushrooms that have been frozen whole; if allowed to thaw naturally they will turn into an unappetizing watery mess. Antonio Carluccio's technique is to immerse whole frozen mushrooms for 2–3 minutes in very hot oil. However, because the melting ice crystals make the hot oil seethe and splutter, it is wise to use a steep-sided pot or wok and to stand well back.

See also the individual recipes for pickling mushrooms and for mushroom duxelles.

Stock

Because some of the recipes in the book call for home-made stock, here are 2 simple recipes, one for chicken, the other for vegetable stock.

Chicken stock

1 uncooked, skinned chicken
  carcass (minus breasts and
  legs)
2 large onions, peeled and
  quartered
2 large carrots, peeled and
  roughly chopped
1 large stick of celery,
  roughly chopped

bunch of fresh parsley (stalks
  and leaves)
12 black peppercorns
2 bay leaves
salt
2 litres (3½ pints) water

Put all the ingredients into a very large pot and bring the water to a boil. Cover, reduce the heat and simmer, skimming off the scum from time to time. After 2 hours, the stock will be ready. Allow it to cool, remove any surplus fat, strain, and refrigerate or pour into freezer bags and store in the deep freeze until required. To thaw, pour boiling water over the frozen stock and carefully peel away the bag. Put the block of frozen stock into a pot, cover and simmer until completely melted.

Vegetable stock

2 onions, peeled
2–3 leeks
3 carrots
5–6 celery stalks
1 parsnip
2 tomatoes
4 tbs olive oil

a few parsley stalks with
  their leaves
1 tbs tomato purée
salt
freshly milled black pepper
2 litres (3½ pints) water

Chop all the vegetables. Put all the ingredients into a pot and bring to the boil. Stir well, cover, reduce the heat and simmer for 1½ hours. Re-season, strain and store as above.

Useful addresses

British Mycological Society
P.O. Box 30
Stourbridge
West Midlands
DY9 9PZ

Mushroom Growers' Association
2 St Paul's Street
Stamford
Lincs PE9 2BE

Residential courses on fungi
FSC Central Services
Field Studies Council
Preston Montford
Montford Bridge
Shrewsbury SY4 1HW

Exotic mushroom growing kits
Wentworth Exotic Mushrooms
1 Hurst Lane
Egham
Surrey TW20 8QJ

Stockists of wild mushrooms and mushroom products
Carluccio's
30 Neal Street
London WC2H 9PS

(Also, Harrods and Harvey Nichols food halls and other specialist outlets)

Select bibliography

Antonio Carluccio, *A Passion for Mushrooms*
(Pavilion, 1989)

Lesley Chamberlain, *The Food and Cooking of Russia*
(Penguin, 1983)

Elizabeth David, *French Provincial Cookery*
(Penguin, 1964)

Patience Grey, *Honey from a Weed*
(Prospect Books, 1986)

Patience Grey and Primrose Boyd, *Plats du Jour*
(Prospect Books, 1990)

Jane Grigson, *The Mushroom Feast*
(Penguin, 1978)

Michael Jordan, *Mushroom Magic*
(Elm Tree, 1989)

Richard Mabey, *Food for Free*
(Fontana, 1975)

Roger Phillips, *Mushrooms and other Fungi of Great Britain and Europe*
(Pan, 1981)

Roger Phillips, *Wild Food*
(Pan, 1983)

Reay Tannahill, *Food in History*
(Penguin, 1988)

The Mycologist
(monthly journal of the British Mycological Society, available on
subscription only; see address on p. 115)

Index